THE LIGHTHOUSES
&
LIGHTSHIPS
OF
CASCO BAY

THE LIGHTHOUSES
&
LIGHTSHIPS
OF
CASCO BAY

PETER DOW BACHELDER

THE PROVINCIAL PRESS
Cape Elizabeth, Maine

First Provincial Press Edition

Front Cover: Photograph by Donald Johnson, Portland, Maine.
Back Cover: Portland Lightship photograph courtesy of the United States Coast Guard. The detail of the painting of Spring Point Ledge Light from the Collection of Howard Reiche, Falmouth, Maine.

ISBN 0-931675-01-4

Library of Congress Cataloging-in-Publication Data

Bachelder, Peter Dow,
    The lighthouses & lightships of Casco Bay / Peter Dow Bachelder
  - 1st Provincial Press edition.
    p. cm.
    Rev. ed. of: Lighthouse of Casco Bay. 1975.
    Includes bibliographical references (p.103-105) and index.
    ISBN 0-931676-01-4
    1. Lighthouses--Maine--Casco Bay--History. 2. Lightships--Maine-
  - Casco Bay--History-- 3. Casco Bay (Me.)--History   I. Bachelder,
    Peter Dow. Lighthouses of Casco Bay. II. Title.
    VK1024.M2B3 1995
    387.1'55'0974191--dc20   95-12006
                                                              CIP

Printed in the United States of America

Dedicated To

*The Keepers of
The Casco Bay Lighthouses*

PREFACE

Casco Bay is a two-hundred-square-mile, island-studded arm of the sea indenting the southern Maine coast between Small Point and Cape Elizabeth. At its western end, it shelters Portland Harbor, the most important port on the coast of Maine. Since the days of its earliest explorers, the harbor (until 1786 called Falmouth) has been widely known as an ice-free, deep-water haven offering spacious, secure anchorage for vessels of all sizes.

Prior to 1650, a markedly successful fishing industry had taken hold here, and during the mid-1700's a lucrative lumber export business — including masts, staves, and timber — dovetailed with a burgeoning West Indies trade, bringing in rum and molasses, to create steady, if not spectacular growth in maritime traffic.

The destruction of Falmouth by British bombardment in 1775 and the subsequent economic slowdown brought about by the American Revolution temporarily strangled this thriving commerce, although when peace returned during the 1780's, so did the flow of shipping. This resurgence foreshadowed an increasingly greater need for ways to protect lives, vessels, and cargoes.

As the eighteenth century drew to a close, persistent local efforts focused the federal government's attention on, then gained its approval for, the first of several navigational aids to mark Portland's harbor and its approaches. Over the next 120 years, the system developed here grew to include six lighthouses and a lightship, each with its own fog signal, not to mention the numerous day marks, beacons, and buoys that ultimately complemented them.

Having grown up and spent much of my early life within sight of one or another of Casco Bay's lighthouses, I almost instinctively developed a keen interest in learning and understanding more about them. The results of my research and studies are summarized in the following outline histories. I shall be more than rewarded if these accounts provide some measure of interest and enjoyment to those who hold any of the fascination for these structures that I do. And I shall be equally pleased if, in the future, those seeking to do further and more detailed research into any facet of their stories finds something useful or meaningful within these pages.

I hasten to point out that the finished work would never have been accomplished without unusually generous assistance from many quarters. Initial acknowledgment must go to Mason Philip Smith, whose boundless knowledge, untiring patience, and endless guidance and counsel through every phase of preparation of this book have been of prime importance; and to his wife, Barbara, who read and reread the original manuscript and offered countless helpful suggestions. Special encouragement also came from Leo Boyle, Lois E. Ewing, Ralph Lewis, Eugene D. Morin, Francis M. O'Brien, Roger O. Peterson, Edward Rowe Snow, Robert L. Sullivan, Susan H. Ward, and Janice A. Wilcox. In particular, I am deeply indebted to Laura L. Anderson, who first encouraged me to consider this project. Later, she turned my uncertain notion of following through on the effort into a formative plan of action. In the final stages of the task, she more than willingly typed and re-typed the myriad additions and changes I was prone to make to successive drafts of the working manuscript.

Special thanks are also in order to Captain Robert A . Lee and his men at the U.S. Coast Guard Base in South Portland; the entire staff of the Portland Public Library; C. C. Church, master photographic lab technician; Glenn B. Skillin, former director at the Maine Historical Society, and his staff; photographer Don Johnson of Portland, whose lenses have chronicled Casco Bay for over 35 years; Howard Reiche of Falmouth, Maine; W. Neil Franklin and Mario D. Fenyo at the National Archives in Washington; Denis Peter Myers of the Historic American Buildings Survey; and Earle G. Shettleworth, Jr. and Kirk Mohney of the Maine Historic Preservation Commission.

Peter Dow Bachelder
Ellsworth, Maine
February, 1995

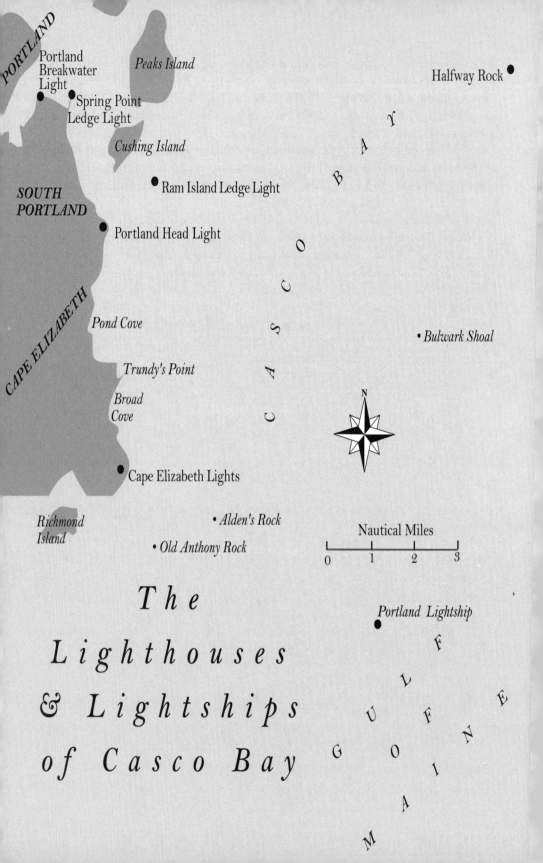

PORTLAND

Portland
Breakwater
Light

Peaks Island

Halfway Rock

Spring Point
Ledge Light

Cushing Island

SOUTH
PORTLAND

Ram Island Ledge Light

Portland Head Light

CAPE ELIZABETH

Pond Cove

Bulwark Shoal

Trundy's Point

Broad
Cove

N

Cape Elizabeth Lights

Richmond
Island

• Alden's Rock

• Old Anthony Rock

Nautical Miles

0   1   2   3

C A S C O   B A Y

Portland Lightship

GULF OF MAINE

The

Lighthouses

& Lightships

of Casco Bay

Contents

INTRODUCTION

The history of lighthouses in the United States dates back to 1715-16 when the first beacon on the continent was erected by the Province of Massachusetts at the entrance to Boston Harbor. This light was supported by duties levied on all incoming and outgoing vessels, except coastwise traffic.

During the next seventy-two years, a total of twelve lighthouses was built by the colonies ranging from Massachusetts southward to South Carolina. At the organization of the federal government in 1789, four others had been undertaken and stood in various stages of completion. These included: Portland Head, Maine; Tybee, at the entrance to the Savannah River, Georgia; Cape Henry, Virginia; and Bald Head, at the entrance to the Cape Fear River, North Carolina.

On August 7, 1789, the maintenance of all navigational aids including lighthouses was put in charge of the Bureau of Lighthouses under the jurisdiction of the Treasury Department. The Secretary of the Treasury himself directed its operations. In 1820, this supervision was transferred to the Fifth Auditor of the Treasury.

During the 1830's, Lighthouse Bureau officials sent out a number of inspectors to make detailed investigations of light stations throughout the country. The purpose of the studies was to determine methods for increasing individual station efficiency. These investigations lasted several years and eventually resulted in the formation of the U.S. Lighthouse Board on October 9, 1852. With the Secretary of the Treasury acting as its chairman, the newly-formed board was composed of two Navy officers, two from the Army Corps of Engineers, and two highly-regarded civilians in the scientific field. This group was to oversee an ambitious program that would modernize and set new standards of operation for this country's entire system of navigational aids.

The Lighthouse Board remained in the Treasury Department until July 1, 1903, when it moved under the control of the Department of Commerce & Labor. In 1910, a simpler form of organization called the Bureau of Lighthouses replaced it. On July 1, 1939, President Franklin D. Roosevelt transferred the Lighthouse Bureau's duties to the jurisdiction of the U.S. Coast Guard, where it rests today, within the Department of Transportation.

The type of construction adopted for individual lighthouses varied widely and depended largely on the importance of the light and the foundation conditions. Various types of framed timber or steel skeletal towers were generally adopted for unattended lights. Attended lights, regarded as lighthouses proper, also have many types. A form frequently used for harbor or lake lights was a combined tower and dwelling of timber or brick construction. For the more important lights, the tower was detached from the dwelling. Most of the older towers of this type were built of brick or stone masonry, with stairways, lantern, and other attachments of cast iron (such as is found at Portland Head). Those of more recent times have a structural open framework of wrought iron or steel with an enclosed stairwell in the center. Reinforced concrete towers have also been used.

When not built on rock, the foundations for towers on land sites were usually single slabs of concrete (as at Cape Elizabeth Light) resting upon the ground, which had previously been excavated to the proper depth.

Many lighthouses at the entrances to harbors were built on the ends of breakwaters or pierheads (Portland Breakwater Light). In such cases, the problem was not essentially different from ordinary shore construction, although the weight of the superstructure had to be considered carefully to avoid undue settling of the foundation. Also, the restriction of available space required the lighthouse to be as compact as possible. In the case of lighthouses on submerged sites, the engineering features were important and often presented great difficulties both in design and construction. Where the bottom was rocky or hard, the lighthouse was built directly on the rock or on a pier. When placed on a ledge of rock (Halfway Rock Light and Ram Island Ledge Light), the ledge was usually leveled or stepped as far as practicable and the structure heavily ragbolted to it.

For submarine sites where the bottom was sand, either a pile or caisson foundation was employed. The screw pile was often used during the nineteenth century and consisted of a stake which was bored like an auger into the bottom. The caisson type (Spring Point Ledge Light) usually consisted of a cylinder from twenty to thirty-five feet in diameter, built up of cast-iron plates, and sunk by dredging or by the pneumatic process into the shoal until a firm bearing was attained, after which the interior was solidly filled with concrete. A few caissons have been placed on underwater rocks or ledges.

The earliest type of lighthouse illumination consisted of an open coal or wood fire, or other inflammable materials, such as pitch, burned on a brazier atop the tower. When Boston Light was established in 1716, it is believed to have been illuminated with tallow candles. By the middle of the eighteenth century, lighthouses were using spider lamps which burned fish or whale oil and hung suspended by iron chains from the top of the lantern. Later, groups of three or four lamps arranged in series provided extra illumination. About 1812, sperm oil was introduced and burned in an Argand lamp which employed parabolic reflectors and a magnifier.

Refinements in this system were constantly being made, but these were overshadowed by the introduction of the Fresnel lens to the United States in 1841.

As devised nearly twenty years before by the French physicist Augustin Fresnel, the apparatus consisted of a polyzonal lens enclosing the lamp and placed at its central focus. The lens was created from glass prisms in panels, the central portions of which were refracting only (dioptric) and whose upper and lower portions were both reflecting and refracting (catadioptric). The advantages of this system lie in the great brilliancy the light emits. This is because a large portion of the light given out by the source is concentrated by the prisms into beams useful to the mariner. Fresnel lenses are still in use in today's lighthouses, and are classified according to their order (size). The size is measured using the inside radius or focal distance of the lens (the distance from the center of the light to the inner surface of the lens). The following table shows the various orders of lighthouse lenses:

Order	Millimeters	Inches
First	920	36.2
Second	700	27.6
Third	500	19.7
Three-And-A-Half	325	14.7
Fourth	250	9.8
Fifth	187.5	7.4
Sixth	150	5.9

By 1859, Fresnel lenses had replaced reflectors in nearly all United States lighthouses. Sperm oil still remained as the leading illuminant, but its increased cost brought about by the growing scarcity of whales forced officials to seek out other possibilities. Many were tried, and during the period 1864-1867, lard oil was adopted as standard. It was widely used until 1877, when its own high cost prompted another change. Within ten years kerosene had become the principal illuminant. Electricity was introduced early in the twentieth century, although it was several decades before it reached universal usage.

Along the North Atlantic seaboard, lighthouses have been placed sufficiently close to one another so that a vessel approaching land will always be in sight of at least one light. In order to avoid confusion in identifying the lights at night, each one was given distinct characteristics. Before the introduction of machinery, the original lights were simply fixed in place. Mechanical apparatus was later introduced which enabled all or a part of the lens portion to revolve. By governing the movement of the lens, light and dark periods could be made to occur in accurate sequence and produce any desired characteristic. The basic ones are: *fixed*, showing a continuous steady light; *flashing*, showing a single flash at regular intervals; *fixed and flashing*, showing a fixed light varied at regular intervals by a single flash of greater brilliancy; *group flashing*, showing groups of flashes at regular intervals; *occulting*, showing a steady light suddenly and totally eclipsed by two or more periods of total darkness at regular intervals.

The foregoing refer to lights of one color (generally white). Lights which change color, giving further diversifications, are called *alternating*. The terms "flashing" and "occulting" refer to the relative duration of light and darkness. In a flashing light, the length of the flash is shorter than the duration of the eclipse. In an occulting light, the occultation is shorter than or equal to the duration of light.

The first fog signal in the United States was a cannon, installed at Boston Light in 1719, which was fired when it was necessary to answer the signals of ships in thick weather. Bells were also introduced at an early date. The first ones were comparatively small and were rung by hand to answer vessels. Larger bells, weighing as much as 4,000 pounds, were soon installed and striking machinery, governed by clockwork, was devised for ringing a regular characteristic. Regardless of their size, bells were not sufficiently loud for seacoast use.

Trumpets, sounded by means of compressed air, were installed experimentally as early as 1851. These produced a more penetrating sound than a bell, although they were still not considered completely satisfactory.

As early as 1855, the Lighthouse Board had investigated the use of steam whistles. The first two stations regularly equipped with this arrangement were Maine locations, West Quoddy Head and Cape Elizabeth. Steam provided the most powerful signal then known. Its principal objection was the considerable length of time necessary to place it in operation, especially since fogs often descend quickly and without warning around coastal stations. This drawback led to the development of the air diaphone horn, powered by compressed air, electricity, or steam. Such a system was considerably more effective and possessed a distinct sound. Fog signals today are generally of this type and are provided with governing devices for timing their blasts.

Although its emergence occurred well into the nineteenth century, the age of the active lightship in America is today only a memory. Lasting slightly less than 165 years, it began as an idea which came full circle in the end.

The basic reason for the lightship — or "lightboat" as it originally was called — was to provide a navigational beacon and a fog signal in each of the many locations where it was either impossible or too costly to place a lighthouse, or where a buoy could not be permanently moored. Ironically, though, as breakthroughs in scientific knowhow occurred, it was the lighthouse that ultimately began the process of replacing the lightship.

The first lightship to see service in American waters was stationed off Willoughby Spit in the Elizabeth River, near Norfolk, Virginia, in 1820. A year later, several other "lightboat stations" were established in various tributaries of Chesapeake Bay.

Once these vessels had proven their dependability, it was decided to test their endurance by mooring a similar ship where it would be subjected to the full force of the open ocean. In 1823, federal officials placed a lightboat off Sandy Hook, New Jersey, to mark the main channel leading to the Port of New York. Its unquestioned success paved the way for widespread acceptance of lightship stations in a great many offshore locations. Within twenty years, more than two dozen vessels could be found swinging at anchor up and down the eastern seaboard; and by 1852, their numbers had swelled to forty-two.

Over the next two decades, Lighthouse Board policy placed increasing emphasis on the lighthouse as a primary navigational aid by replacing lightships which had stood in more protected spots, such as harbors or bays, with screw-pile and caisson towers. Yet, more than a century would elapse before the advent of technologically superior, yet less expensive equipment allowed the widespread removal of light vessels that served exposed, "outside" locations.

Slow to appear in New England waters, lightships here were also the last to survive the changeover to more modern modes of illumination. During the 1850's, the Board established the first of more than a dozen sites selected off southern New England shores. At the outbreak of World War I, only two had been eliminated. Throughout the nineteenth century, however, no light vessel ever saw service north of Boston.

In March 1903, Lightship No. 74 took up newly-established station off Portland (Maine) Harbor. It was to be the single such location along the Maine coast — in fact, the only one between Boston Harbor and Lurcher Shoal, New Brunswick.

During the mid-twentieth century, large unmanned buoys became part of the federal government's basic cost-saving strategy within its overall implementation plan to phase out all still-active lightships. As early as 1938, one replaced the Heald Bank (Texas) lightship, an occasion which clearly signaled the beginning of the end for these traditionally-crewed vessels.

By the 1960's, the Coast Guard had begun employing massive three- and four-legged skeletal structures, similar in design to the "Texas" towers then being used in oil-drilling operations across the Gulf of Mexico. These were essentially huge platforms standing on steel-pile foundations. The first such tower replaced the Buzzards Bay (Massachusetts) lightship in November 1961, and six more went into use along the east coast during the next few years.

Another successful approach involved the use of electronically automated large navigational buoys (LNB's). An experimental type replaced the Scotland lightship near Sandy Hook, New Jersey, during the late 1960's. It became the prototype for several working models which were soon deployed along both Atlantic and Pacific coasts. Able to provide nearly all the services of a manned lightship at a small fraction of its operating costs, the LNB ultimately proved to be not only the most economical replacement, but also the most reliable from the standpoint of maintenance even in the most exposed positions. It was this type of buoy that eventually was chosen to take over the Portland station.

It has been fifty-five years now since the Coast Guard has been in charge of navigational aids across the country. In the true spirit of this fine organization, its members have continued the noteworthy traditions previously achieved by the hardy breed of Lighthouse Service technicians who performed their too-often thankless tasks for nearly a century and a half.

During the past generation, rapid advances in technology have enabled highly sophisticated, vastly more efficient, yet relatively inexpensive hardware to operate lights, fog signals, buoys, and all manner of navigational aids independent of human control. This process of automation has essentially dehumanized the long-traditional task of "keeping the lights." Today, Casco Bay's functional lighthouses are each operated electronically and require only periodic maintenance to keep them providing the highest degree of safety yet known to mariners. Although the age of lighthouse keepers is gone forever here, the countless hours given by these faithful individuals will never reveal the myriad acts of bravery and devotion they performed in the line of duty. The dedication of this book to them can only be an insignificant tribute to both the men and their labors.

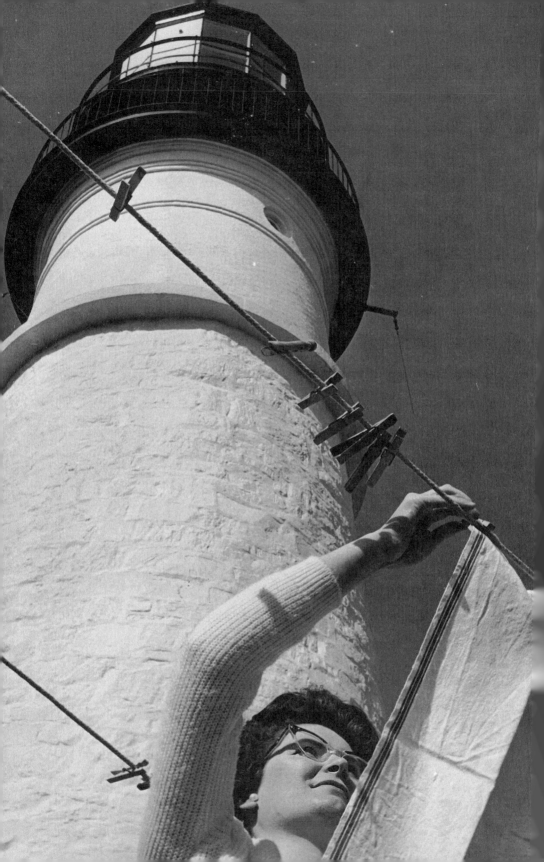

CHAPTER ONE

PORTLAND HEAD LIGHT

As a tourist attraction, Portland Head Light has few equals. Photographers make gaudy calendars and post cards attempting to capture one or another of its ever-changing moods. Tour and travel guides paint glowing word-pictures proclaiming its many charms. During the last decade alone, more than a half million visitors journeyed to view and admire it in the simple beauty of its surroundings. The very fact that it is Maine's oldest lighthouse has helped transform this stately structure into a living symbol of Maine's maritime heritage, a romantic connection between its rugged past and the present.

Portland Head Light's existence spans more than two centuries, nearly preceding the birth of the very nation it serves. The American Revolution achieved independence for a ragged band of colonies, determined to think and act for themselves; and while it won them the freedoms they had sought, it also forced upon them the process of transformation from colonies to states. For most the shift was rapid. Within a year of the Declaration of Independence, ten states had drawn up their own constitutions. In Massachusetts, of which the District of Maine was a part, the transition was much more slow and deliberate, although ultimately as effective as any. The Massachusetts State Constitution, adopted June 15, 1780, showed much of the common sense attributed even then to New Englanders.

One of the immediate problems facing each of the new states was foreign trade. Due to measures previously adopted by Great Britain, all West Indies ports had been closed to American vessels, denying them the profitable trade they had enjoyed before the war. At the same time, British shipping was allowed free use of American ports and became the chief carrier of its produce, causing incalculable damage to the struggling American economy.

Left: Portland photographer Don Johnson's lens has captured a keeper's wife hanging out her laundry at Portland Head Light in 1961.

These policies had been seriously felt in New England, center for the lucrative rum trade and booming lumber business. Almost immediately, concerned individuals began urging the Massachusetts Legislature to adopt some measures of protection. On October 22, 1783, the General Court pushed through a resolution which required shipping entering any of its ports to pay a lighthouse duty. The levy, amounting to two pence a ton for vessels weighing up to thirty tons and four pence a ton for those heavier than that, was to be used among other things to maintain the Commonwealth's five then-existing lighthouses. To protect its own interests, the court added an exclusion clause exempting vessels engaged either in coastwise trade or the fishing business.

Maine interests were disturbed by this law, primarily because no lighthouse marked their shores, which meant they would doubtless fail to benefit by it. In 1784 a petition by seventy-four owners and masters of vessels in Cumberland County, encompassing Casco Bay, went to the General Court in Boston seeking a lighthouse for their area. Nothing happened. The following spring, residents of Falmouth, renamed Portland in 1786, banded together in a move for positive action. They approached Mr. Joseph Noyes, their personal represen-

A storm at Portland Head Light station in the 1960's. Ram Island Ledge Light is in the right background.

Don Johnson

Installed in 1855, this cast iron staircase winds from ground level to the lantern deck inside the tower at Portland Head Light.

tative to the General Court, and asked him to procure passage of a law excluding British ships from becoming carriers of American commodities by imposing duties on exports shipped by them. In addition, they repeated the previous request for a lighthouse, suggesting Portland Head as a likely location. Noyes carried the demands to Boston, but the court, noting the Commonwealth's depressed economic state, refused to cooperate and the matter was dropped.

Then an incident off Portland's outer harbor early in 1787 provided the catalytic effect that three years of human eloquence had failed to provoke. On Sunday evening, February 4, a ninety-ton sloop, southbound from Sheepscot to Newbury, Massachusetts, was wrecked on the fourth point of Bangs (now Cushing) Island, less than a mile from Portland Head.

Her captain, Moses Chase, and a boy named John Deane were drowned. The rest of her five-man crew managed to save themselves by clinging to floating wreckage. The following week the *Cumberland Gazette*, Portland's only newspaper, commented:

> "Does not this unhappy accident evince the necessity of having a Lighthouse at the entrance of the harbor? It is supposed that the loss of this vessel was occasioned by the want of one."

Collection: Earle G. Shettleworth

Members of the Venerable Cunner Association & Propeller Club during their outing at Portland Head on August 3, 1858. The light station consists of the 1817 keeper's dwelling; the rubble-work tower; and the 24-foot wood-frame bell tower and 1,500-pound cast-iron bell.

In the weeks that followed, Portland area citizens circulated another petition for a light. This time they forced a small appropriation amounting to about $750, although very little was ever accomplished before the job had to be suspended for lack of additional funds.

On April 30, 1789, George Washington became the first president of the fledgling United States of America. A few weeks previously, the new nation's first congress had assembled in New York City. Among the measures adopted there during that historic summer session was one, approved August 7, 1789, which provided that those expenses:

> "In the necessary support, maintenance and repairs of all
> lighthouses, beacons, buoys and public piers erected, placed,
> or sunk before the passing of this act, at the entrance of, or
> within any bay, inlet, harbor, or port of the United States,
> for rendering the navigation thereof easy and safe, shall be
> defrayed out of the Treasury of the United States."

In a document signed in the House of Representatives June 9, 1790, and in the Senate a day later, the Commonwealth of Massachusetts ceded six lighthouses, including the unfinished Portland Head Light, to the federal government, with the provision that:

> "If the United States shall at any time hereafter neglect
> to keep lighted, and in repair, any one or more of the light
> houses aforesaid, then the grant of such lighthouse or light
> houses so neglected shall be void and no effect."

Within two months, a $1,500 congressional appropriation had been made to resume construction of Portland Head Light, and Secretary of the Treasury

Alexander Hamilton authorized funds "to cause the said lighthouse to be finished." Hamilton appointed General Benjamin Lincoln, Collector of the Port of Boston and in charge of all lights in the Commonwealth, to superintend construction for the government. Portland masons John Nichols and Jonathan Bryant received the contract to build the tower.

Their building material consisted of field stones, weighing from ten pounds apiece to as much as they could lift. These were gathered in nearby fields, placed on a drag and hauled to the site by oxen. This rubble-stone, as it was called, was then set in lime, formed from limestone quarried in Rockland, sailed to Portland and landed at Bryant's lime kiln near the foot of India Street.

Plans for the light originally had called for it to surmount a fifty-eight foot tower, but when a government inspection team determined that at this height a nearby headland would block its rays to the south, they were altered to raise the structure to seventy-two feet. This decision caused a row between Bryant and General Lincoln. Bryant resigned in a huff, leaving Nichols to complete the task on his own, which he did, finishing November 9, 1790.

The additional fourteen feet of stone work reduced the tower's topmost diameter to less than six feet, which made it too small to accommodate the proposed lantern cage and lens assembly. Smaller ones were secured and installed, and the station went into operation at sunset January 10, 1791.

Three days previously, President Washington had personally appointed Captain Joseph Greenleaf keeper of the new light. Both Greenleaf and Barzillai Delano, a blacksmith from nearby Pond Cove, had been under final consideration for the post, but it was awarded to Greenleaf because of his prior service in the Continental Army.

Captain Greenleaf was given a home near the light, although for two and one-

Below: Portland Head Light station appeared this way during 1883-84.

Collection: Maine Historical Society

With twenty feet added to its height, the lighthouse at Portland Head stood as above from 1865 until 1883. The pyramidal bell tower was relegated to standby status in 1872 by the station's first fog horn, which was placed atop the small wooden engine house to the left of the light tower.

half years he received no salary. Beginning July 1, 1793, the government allowed him "160 doll(ars)" a year. His career ended abruptly October 3, 1795. While crossing Fore River (between Cape Elizabeth and Portland), in a small boat he died of a stroke. His position was filled by David Duncan, who served only a year before yielding to Barzillai Delano, who had vied with Greenleaf for the post more than five years earlier.

The treacherous ledges over which the new light prevailed claimed two small schooners during late fall storminess in 1798. On November 26, a vessel went to pieces below the light. Three weeks later to the day, another schooner came ashore at the same place. In an heroic effort, the captain's son braved the icy waters and swam ashore with a line, enabling those still aboard to reach land safely.

Around the turn of the nineteenth century, Portland Head Light came under fire from General Lincoln in Boston. During one of his inspection tours Lincoln discovered that the stone tower was allowing excessive amounts of dampness inside. His later written report recommended having the entire tower sheathed with pine planking, secured by iron hoops. "Well-painted" wooden shingles, overlaying the planking, would complete the change. So far as is known, however, this idea was never carried out.

As the years passed, the dampness problem intensified. During the fall of

1810, General Henry A. S. Dearborn, Superintendent of Lighthouses for the Commonwealth of Massachusetts, inspected the station. By this time, much of the timber flooring within the tower had completely rotted and was in serious danger of collapse. Dearborn arranged for its immediate replacement, but because Delano had stored the coming winter's lantern-oil supply about the floor, and moving it around seemed more dangerous than leaving it alone, the repairs were left until the following spring.

The station's first major physical change occurred in 1813. At the suggestion of Winslow Lewis, respected for his advances in illuminating apparatus, twenty-five feet of the tower's stonework were removed. A new timber decking, sheathed in copper, was then laid over the forty-seven foot shell and made ready to receive a ten-foot octagonal iron lantern cage. Following Lewis' carefully worded instructions, the cage was "glassed with the best double glass of the Boston Glass House Manufacture." Finished in June, the remodeling cost a total of $2,100.

Further change came three years later. A contract drawn up in September 1816 and awarded to Henry Dyer II of Cape Elizabeth, gave him until October the following year to erect a one-story dwelling house, thirty-four feet by twenty feet, that would accommodate the keeper. The completed structure was to be divided into two main rooms, with a cellar ten feet by twelve feet beneath, and a porch in the rear. Dyer completed the job ahead of schedule and Barzillai Delano moved in during the fall.

The bark *Annie C. Maguire* rammed ashore against the ledges at Portland Head on December 24, 1886. *Collection: Maine Historical Society*

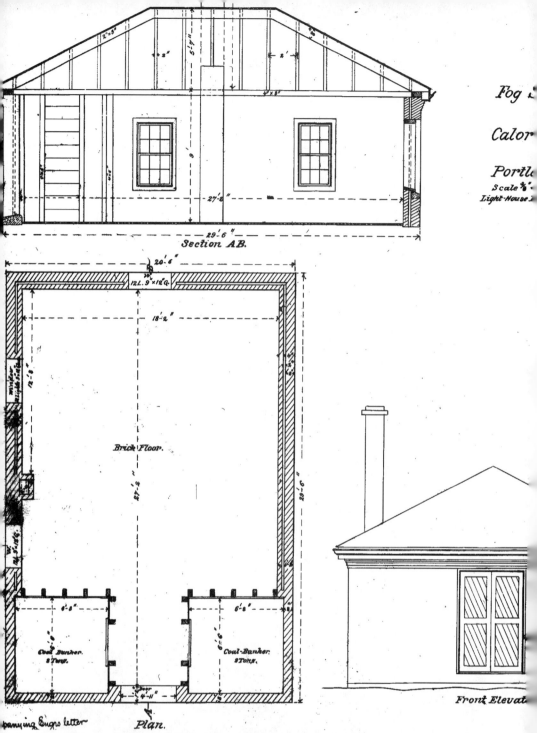

Section AB.

Plan.

Brick Floor.

Coal Bunker.
8 Tons.

Coal Bunker.
8 Tons.

Fog

Calor

Portl
Scale ⅜
Light-House

Front Elevat

Historic American Buildings Survey

In 1888 plans for a new fog signal house were carried out at Portland Head. A brick building, about twenty feet by thirty feet, was constructed where the smaller engine house had stood.

U.S. Coast Guard photo

The Portland Head station as it appeared in 1890.

In 1820, the State of Maine received its independence from Massachusetts. A Treasury Department letter to Boston's Henry Dearborn dated March 29, 1821, informed him:

> "As the District of Maine has been admitted into the Union as an independent state, its relation to the United States has undergone a change which renders it proper that the several offices of the United States within it should be confided to its citizens. The supeintendence of the Lighthouse establishment, therefore, with which you have theretofore been charged, within the limits of that state, has been transferred to Isaac Ilsley, Esq., the Collector of the Customs at Portland.... Your agency in regard to the Light House establishment will consequently be confined to Massachusetts Proper. You will be pleased to communicate with Mr. Ilsley such information now committed to him as you think of advantage, and to instruct the several Keepers of Light Houses within the state of Maine to make all necessary communications and return to him."

Before the year was out, Barzillai Delano died in service and Joshua Freeman became the new keeper. During his twenty-year tour of duty, no major changes were carried out at the station. Through no fault of Freemen, several disasters

Collection: *William B. Jordan, Jr.*

ABOVE: The frigate *U.S.S. Constitution*, shown here under tow, passes Portland Head after a July 1931 visit to Portland

BELOW: The *S.S. Jeremiah O'Brien*, one of two World War II Liberty ships still afloat, steams toward Portland Head as it makes its way into Portland Harbor in August of 1994. The *O'Brien* stopped in Portland en route to its home port of San Francisco following a visit to the D-Day invasion beaches of France's Normandy coast.

Don Johnson Photo

occurred almost at his doorstep. The schooner *President* and the ship *Macedonia* were both lost beneath the light. In 1831, the bark *North Star* went to pieces in nearby Ship Cove, less than one-quarter of a mile away.

Richard Lee assumed the keeper's duties in 1840, following Joshua Freeman's retirement. Lee was succeeded in 1849 by John Watts. During the latter's tenure, the light underwent considerable alteration. In August 1850 the lantern cage, weatherbeaten and full of leaks, was taken down. New Fresnel lenses from France were installed and a lantern casing, manufactured in Portland, went into use.

Then in June 1852, inspection by officials from District Headquarters in Boston revealed several unusual happenings at the station. In less than two years' time the reflectors in the lantern had somehow become badly scratched and the station was operating a private fog horn, which was being blown only for certain vessels as a result of a private agreement between Watts and their captains.

The resulting report touched off a complex series of changes lasting nearly thirty years, which ultimately brought the station to the highly efficient level of operation it has maintained since. In the year and a half immediately following, three new keepers were tried before the new U. S. Lighthouse Board, organized October 9, 1852, decided in favor of James Delano, Barzillai's son. In 1855, the Board built a twenty-four foot wooden skeletal frame tower on the point south of the light tower, and in it hung a 1,500-pound cast iron bell, transferred from the Cape Elizabeth station. At the same time, it oversaw minor repairs to the base of the tower.

The shocking loss of the iron steamship *Bohemian* off Cape Elizabeth in February 1864 played a major role in having Portland Head's light tower raised twenty feet later the same year. A set of second-order Fresnel lenses replaced the fourth-order ones installed the previous decade. Behind the lenses, a new five-wick lamp completed a changeover from sperm oil to kerosene. The elevated tower and its improved lighting arrangement went into service December 20, 1864.

The great September gale of 1869, responsible for the loss of at least twenty vessels and an unknown number of lives in Casco Bay, did not spare Portland Head. Madcap waves tore loose the big fog bell and flung it into a cleft in the rocks below the light. Consequently a new pyramidal bell tower, complete with a 2,000-pound bell and Stevens striker, went up the next year where the older one had stood. The newer bell saw only three years of regular service before a large trumpet, used previously at Monhegan Island, was transferred to Portland Head, becoming the station's first official fog horn. To provide steam to blow the horn, a small one-story engine house was built on the site of the 1870 bell tower. The big iron bell was rehung nearby and relegated to standby status. Two years later, the trumpet was removed in favor of a second-class horn.

The establishment of Halfway Rock Light station, ten miles east of Portland,

Collection: William B. Jordan, Jr.

One of Portland Head Light's most colorful and popular keepers was Joseph Woodbury Strout, here posed at the station with his daughter Martha.

Collection: Peter Dow Bachelder

Head keeper Frank Hilt works from a basket while whitewashing Portland Head's light tower in 1935, an annual task usually performed during late spring. Twenty years later, workmen from Boston sandblasted the stone shaft down to bare rock and mortar and applied the first-ever coat of paint, a plastic-vinyl compound designed to resist weathering.

in 1871 prompted the Lighthouse Board to reconsider the importance of the Portland Head station. In 1882, it decided to shorten the tower twenty feet and reinstall a fourth-class lantern. Carried out in 1883, the move caused vigorous opposition, forcing the Board to reinstate the tower to its former height the very next year. While this was being done, a broader platform was mounted atop the tower and another, larger lantern with a more powerful lens was installed. The new apparatus went into use January 15, 1885. The tower with these improvements stands today in relatively this same state.

In 1869, Joshua Strout became Portland Head Light's eleventh keeper, beginning a thirty-five year stay. During his tenure, he came to be loved and admired by his many friends and associates, as well as by the countless visitors to the station. A dedicated and courageous man, Captain Strout should also be remembered for his heroic acts in saving the crew of the three-masted bark *Annie C. Maguire*, which landed against the rocks beneath the light December 24, 1886.

Leaving Buenos Aires, Argentina early in December that year, the thirty-four year old *Annie C. Maguire,* formerly the clipper bark *Golden State,* headed north in ballast toward Portland. A short time after her departure, Kidder, Peabody & Company, Boston bankers, notified the sheriff in Portland to be on the watch for the vessel. Her owners, the D. & J. Maguire Company of Quebec, had gone into debt and authorities had been advised to attach the bark as soon as she reached American waters. But there was no need to go in search of the *Annie Maguire.* Shortly before midnight Christmas Eve, the aged vessel piled onto the ledges at Portland Head, only a stone's throw from the lighthouse.

Surviving accounts of the wreck often mention a swirling blizzard which caused Captain O'Neil, *Annie's* master, to misjudge his distance from shore.

Actual Weather Bureau journals show a different story. They indicate the temperature at the time of the disaster was a balmy forty-six degrees. A little light rain had been observed falling through a southerly breeze, but seas were reported as only moderate and the visibility was remarkably good. The bark's shuddering impact with the shore created a jolt which shook the entire light station. Rushing outside with his son Joseph, Captain Strout could make out the *Annie C. Maguire's* ghostly form lying broadside to the ledges, while the rays from the big light above played an eerie scene on her flapping sails.

Working calmly in the face of potential disaster, Strout and his son flung a length of rope aboard the helpless bark. While the *Maguire's* crew fastened their end in the crosstrees, the elder Strout wrapped the other end around the base of the light tower. The line, together with a twenty-five foot board laid across the rocks, enabled him to bring the *Annie Maguire's* fifteen-man crew, including Captain O'Neil's wife and two young children, ashore unharmed.

Daylight Christmas morning showed a gaping hole in *Annie's* undersides which precluded any thoughts of her successful salvage. The rising tides filled her old hull, and the vengeful waves played havoc with her broken frame.

Left: An air-diaphragm chime horn, placed atop a steel-frame tower, became Portland Head's new fog signal in 1938.   *U.S. Coast Guard*

Below: Weakened in 1962, the whistle house succumbed to an April 1975 pounding which necessitated its being razed and replaced.

Portland Evening Express

Portland Evening Express

Debris litters the Portland Head station's lawn in the wake of the April 3, 1975 gale.

At an auction held in Portland December 29, Thomas Towle purchased the wreck for $177.50 and subsequently stripped the vessel of most of her rigging and fixtures. Before he could do more, a storm on New Year's Day 1887 broke up the *Maguire's* remains and strewed her wreckage for miles. Today, a hand-lettered inscription painted on the rocks below the station calls attention to the unfortunate night the *Annie C. Maguire* came ashore.

Further refinements at the fog signal station adjacent to the light occurred in August 1887 with the addition of a 24-inch caloric engine. This machine, which had powered a ten-inch steam whistle at Boston Light for three years, was soon found ineffective, however, and a new diesel engine replaced it. At this, the trumpet from Monhegan Island, used as a standby for the previous decade, returned to active service. Later it was replaced by another stronger one which stood until 1938.

In the seventy-fifth year of its existence, the original two-room stone dwelling house was demolished, and during the early months of 1891 the Lighthouse Board administered the construction of a larger wooden building, designed and fitted to accommodate the families of both head and assistant keepers.

The outbreak of the Spanish-American War caused Portland Head Light to be extinguished April 30, 1898, as a precautionary measure against the possible onset of Spanish Naval activity along the North Atlantic coast. When the threat failed to materialize, its lamps were again lighted during the latter part of July.

In 1900, the rubble tower received its most extensive renovation of this century. Many of its stones were removed and replaced, and the entire structure was set in mortar. At the fog signal house, two four-horsepower oil engines with air compressors were installed, and a cooling tank was built. The same year, the station itself was connected to the public water supply from Portland, which required laying 500 feet of pipe.

Joshua Strout's retirement in 1904 due to illness prompted the appointment of his son, Joseph, as head keeper. An assistant to his father for nearly thirty years, the younger Strout carried on the popular family's regime in traditional fashion until 1928, when poor health forced him to step down.

When a crack appeared in it in 1931, the old English-cast fog bell was retired, and a new one from Lighthouse Headquarters, Staten Island, was delivered in January 1932. At the time of its removal, the English bell was said to be one of the oldest and probably the only one of its type then in service. Cast in 1867, it had survived 62 years of duty, including an unexpected dunking in the ocean during a December 1898 gale.

Fog, which often shrouds Casco Bay and makes the movement of oceangoing traffic hazardous at best, proved fatal to the auxiliary schooner *Lochinvar*, Captain Frank Doughty, on October 4, 1932. Inbound with 40,000 pounds of fresh haddock, Captain Doughty misjudged his distance from the Cape shore and his vessel struck an offshore ledge near where the *Annie Maguire* had been lost. Lifesavers, dispatched from Two Lights, picked up the *Lochinvar's* fourteen-man crew, who had scarcely been able to get away from their ship before she went down.

The fog signal was again modernized during April 1938 when a new air-diaphragm chime horn, complete with electrically-driven air equipment, replaced the first-class trumpet. The new signal, a three-horn apparatus, was placed atop a steel-frame tower near the northeast corner of the "whistle" house and rigged to emit a four-second blast every twenty seconds.

On July 1, 1939, the duties of the Bureau of Lighthouses, which in 1910 had succeeded the former Lighthouse Board, were absorbed by the U. S. Coast Guard. When the changeover came, Captain Frank Hilt was keeping the light at Portland Head, assisted by Robert Thayer Sterling. Hilt stayed on until 1943, when Sterling replaced him; but with the latter's retirement in May 1946, the days of civilian keepers at the station had gone forever.

Portland Head Light and station - January 1995.

With United States involvement in World War II, most illuminated Atlantic coast navigational aids were extinguished in deference to German submarine activity. The beacon on Portland Head dimmed and went out June 27, 1942, while the fog signal went silent July 5th. Keepers Hilt and Sterling maintained the darkened station with all the attention it deserved under normal conditions, although the equipment was not turned on again until June 29, 1945.

Visitors to the station during the summer of 1955 caught an unusual view of the old stone tower. That year a Boston firm sandblasted its surface clean, exposing the original gray appearance. In September, workmen applied the first coat of paint the shaft had ever known, a white plastic-vinyl mixture especially designed to withstand the extremes of weathering it would have to endure. Present-day maintenance calls for the tower to get an annual stripping, usually in the spring, whereupon a fresh coat of paint is administered.

Electricity, first installed in 1929, powers the present lantern, an airways-type beacon installed during the summer of 1958 under a Coast Guard appropriation of $4,450. It has four prismatic lenses which rotate upon an electrically-powered shaft and magnify two 1000-watt lamps to 200,000 candlepower. A flashing white beam pours out from 101 feet above the ocean, and under optimum conditions may be seen from as many as thirty miles at sea.

Through the years, Mother Nature has continued to wreak havoc on the station and its equipment. During the great Cape Elizabeth gale of March 3, 1947, the fifteen-year-old fog bell was torn from its mooring and clattered to the base of the cliffs below. In December 1962, a series of monstrous waves cracked three walls of the engine house, tore off part of the bulkhead door to the main cellar, and ripped away quantities of shingles from each of the buildings. Then on April 3, 1975, the sea's relentless force battered in the southeastern wall of the whistle house, completing the destruction it had nearly caused earlier. In the process, it knocked out the station's fog horn and extinguished her beacon. A crew of firemen was called to the scene when diesel fuel leaked from storage tanks and station personnel became concerned that fallen power cables nearby might cause a flash fire.

Power to the lighthouse beacon was soon restored. The fog signal had to be replaced, though, because the air compressors controlling it had been ruined. A temporary horn, one with a high, electronic, ear-shattering tone, acted as substitute until a permanent one, previously used at Halfway Rock, could be airlifted to the site and installed.

Prompted by ever-escalating costs of maintaining manned light stations and the advent of inexpensive, labor saving technology — including photoelectric cells to turn lights on and off, and radio sensors to detect the presence of fog — the federal government in 1968 mandated the Coast Guard to automate more than 400 lighthouses, lightships, and other aids to navigation by 1990.

During the fall of 1985, Coast Guard officials in Washington announced that 107 lighthouses had been automated, allowing a personnel reduction of 268

Don Johnson Photo

Sunrise at Portland Head Light.

and prompting an annual cost savings of $45 million. In the First District, stretching north from Watch Hill, Rhode Island to include the Massachusetts, New Hampshire, and Maine coasts, all but 32 lighthouses had been automated and decommissioned. Less than two years later, the number had shrunk to sixteen.

Portland Head's turn finally came in 1989. A crowd of some 600 people attended a ceremony marking the automation of the nearly 200-year-old station.

Many months previous, local residents had been debating the possible fate of the site once Coast Guard personnel were gone. The idea of using the station as a national lighthouse museum initially seemed to have some merit — and support — although townspeople later over whelmingly rejected it in favor of a smaller such enterprise, one that would limit its scope to a history of the local light station.

The Cape Elizabeth town council approved this more limited concept in October 1989. Early in 1991, proponents of the effort began a fund-raising drive to support the museum. Following extensive renovation at the light station, the Museum at Portland Head opened in July 1992.

Today's casual visitor to Portland Head drives over a smooth, arcing, blacktop roadway, through the peaceful grounds of the former Fort Williams, once a major Army installation dating back prior to the Spanish-American War. Now the property of the town of Cape Elizabeth, its sleepy atmosphere adds a blend of dignity and romance to the scenic surroundings. The easy accessibility to the lighthouse makes it hard to imagine earlier times when Portland Head was an isolated outpost surrounded by dense thickets and woods; and the station's keepers saw nothing charming about the location, as they faithfully performed their ongoing task of guiding ships safely past its treacherous shores.

CHAPTER TWO

THE CAPE ELIZABETH LIGHTS

The first landfall for marine traffic seeking Portland Harbor is an outlying section of Cape Elizabeth long popularly known as "Two Lights," a name derived from twin lighthouses erected there in 1828. Both towers survive today, overlooking a grassy ridge which meets the sea at a spot variously called Lighthouse Point and Boathouse Point; although in recent years only one light has been operational.

Because of the location's prominence, the federal government in 1811 decided to mark it for the mariners' benefit. That spring, Massachusetts Lighthouse Superintendent General Henry Dearborn surveyed the area and purchased a tract of land costing eighty dollars from Edward and Enoch Dyer, owners of adjoining farms along the southern extremity of the Cape. On July 24, government engineers negotiated a contract with Edward Robinson and John P. Bartlett, both Portland men, who agreed to put up a stone monument on the crest of the ridge. Robinson and Bartlett in turn arranged with the Dyers for them to furnish the necessary building materials.

Beginning the first week in August, the two contractors completed their task November 30. Constructed according to their contract, "of the best undressed stone" set in lime, the finished monument stood forty-five feet high. It had been shaped in the form of an octagonal pyramid and mounted atop an octagonal water table. At the pinnacle of the column, 125 feet above sea level, rested a three-foot capstone, actually just an ordinary boulder taken from a nearby field, as were the other stones that comprised the tower. The entire structure received a coat of paint—the lower half white and the upper section black.

As if to accentuate the need for a navigational aid here, the wood-laden sloop *Resolution* ran ashore October 24, 1811, within sight of the unfinished column. Both vessel and cargo became a total loss.

Built in 1811, this rubble-stone monument stood where the present Cape Elizabeth Light stands today.

During the next fifteen years, shipping past the end of the Cape increased dramatically, prompting repeated complaints from unhappy captains and sailors that although the stone monument served well as a day marker, some sort of beacon should be added as a nighttime guide. Consequently, formal written word from Isaac Ilsley, Collector of the Customs in Portland, reached Stephen Pleasonton, Fifth Auditor of the Treasury in Washington, who had charge of all lighthouse construction. To the delight of all concerned, Pleasonton approved a lighthouse on Cape Elizabeth late in 1827.

The following spring, government officials acquired twelve more acres of land and in June awarded a contract to Jeremiah Berry for him to build not just one, but two, square rubble-stone towers to cost $4,250. Under terms of the arrangement, Berry also agreed to take down the old monument before starting any new construction.

Within four months, twin towers stood along the ridge, three hundred yards apart, in roughly an east-west line. The lights, nearly 140 feet above sea level, were first illuminated officially October 28, 1828. Standing where the 1811 column had been, the east tower showed a fixed white light. The west tower beamed an occulting light with a ninety second pattern — forty-five seconds of light followed by forty-five seconds of darkness.

President John Quincy Adams appointed the first keeper, Elisha Jordan, who received an annual salary of $450 and strict orders to make his job a full time responsibility. Told he must live at the station, he was advised he "must make it a habit to be at home." Jordan remained as keeper until 1834, when he was replaced by Charles Staples.

The acquisition of a new lantern cage for the west light in June 1850 marked the first in a series of significant improvements at the station during the next few years. On August 21, 1852, Congress appropriated $2,500 for installation of a fog bell with accompanying bell-house and striker machinery. Two years later Fresnel lenses replaced the parabolic reflectors in each lantern. These lenses, designed by the French physicist Augustin Jean Fresnel, had recently revolutionized the whole mode of lighthouse illumination by employing compound lenses rather than ordinary mirrors, thereby producing a much more brilliant light.

Almost as soon as this latest change had been made, a public notice in December 1854 proclaimed that on June 1 the following year, the west light would be permanently discontinued and the east light converted to an occulting beacon. The newly organized U.S. Lighthouse Board had recommended the change, stating that the west tower's revolving light was visible over a much greater distance than the fixed light. The Board maintained that during the period when a vessel had sighted only the revolving beacon, there was no way to distinguish it from Wood Island Light, off the Saco River, nine miles to the southwest.

The reasoning was sound, although it failed to prevent bitter opposition from local mariners. Their objections delayed the light's removal several weeks, but its lantern was eventually turned off August 1, 1855. At this, a great public outcry arose that subsided only after the second beacon had been restored and both lights had reverted to their former status. As an alternate method of clarification, Wood Island Light was rebuilt in 1858 and the characteristic of its

Nineteenth century Portland artist Harrison Bird Brown painted this scene of a shipwreck along the Cape Elizabeth shore.

Collection: Howard Reiche

beacon was changed to occulting red.

Despite these efforts to improve the Cape station's effectiveness, shipping locally continued to have its problems. In mid–March 1857, the bark *Tasmania* arrived in Portland from Liverpool to load supplies before sailing for Nassau. She put to sea again the evening of the 19th. A dense fog blanketed the coast as Captain Stickney eased his 386-ton vessel past Portland Head and Trundy's Reef. Watching intently for a glimpse of the lights on the end of the Cape, Stickney unwittingly brought the *Tasmania* closer to shore than he intended. The bark glided noiselessly toward Broad Cove and a moment later struck the rocky beach, shattering her hull.

With no wind and a flat sea, the *Tasmania* was in no immediate danger. Captain Stickney sent a party below to determine the extent of any damage while he contemplated methods of refloating his ship. But when he learned the bark's entire bottom had been knocked out, he realized the vessel must certainly die where she lay. In the darkness, a dejected captain and his crew went ashore. After stripping her of sails and rigging the following day, Stickney abandoned the broken bark. Her cargo of iron and crockery was later rescued unharmed, although a consignment of salt was destroyed when the rising tide got into it.

One year later, the schooner *Abigail* sailed to her doom practically beneath the eastern light. She had come in from the east, and manuevering in a thick fog had missed the harbor's entrance, ending up stranded on the rocks at the high tide mark where she went to pieces within two days. In 1861, the little schooner *Susan* drove ashore on Dyer's Point, just a few hundred yards from the station. She, too, became a total loss.

Shortly before the close of the Civil War, officials in Washington thought that further identification was needed for the Cape lights, so the west tower was painted with one broad, vertical red stripe on its southern or seaward face. The east tower received four horizontal red bands. The logic here is difficult to understand, since there was no other twin tower station in either direction along the coast for sixty miles, the nearest ones being Matinicus Rock to the north and the Cape Ann Lights in Massachusetts to the south.

In 1869, the Lighthouse Board began experimenting with steam to power fog signals, selecting two Maine stations, Cape Elizabeth and West Quoddy Head, as the first to receive and try the new equipment. That year, it erected a small wooden building on Dyer's Point, near the shore south of the lights, to house a boiler that would power a ten-inch steam locomotive whistle. The apparatus was then calibrated to emit an eight-second blast once each minute during foggy weather. On their first tour of the station following its installation, the Board's inspectors heartily endorsed its performance.

Left: One of twin square rubble-stone towers, this is the western tower of the Cape Elizabeth Lights as it appeared in 1855.

National Archives

Not so gratifying to them was the condition of the two towers. They had fallen into such disrepair, the only alternative in their minds was to have them re-built. As a result, the inspecting committee sought an appropriation for that purpose. The request was denied, but was repeated in 1870 and again in 1871. Despite the Board's persistence, legislators weren't prepared to endorse the change until they had seen and studied a more detailed independent report. In 1872, a team of engineers arrived in Cape Elizabeth to examine the stone tow-ers and report their findings.

Contrary to the inspectors' wishes, the engineers' study recommended that only the west tower should be replaced. On March 3, 1873, Congress approved the plan and made available $30,000 to accomplish it. But with that amount, the Board found it could afford to have the east tower rebuilt, as well. During the ensuing twelve months, the old stone columns were taken down and re-placed with two sixty-five foot cast-iron shells lined inside with brick. The curved casings had been molded in sections by the local Portland Machine Works. When completed in 1874, the new towers received a coat of brown paint, since it was felt this would save on upkeep.

As soon as the new lighthouses were ready for service, the lighting devices from the rubble-stone towers were transferred to the newer ones and the char-acteristic of each beacon was altered. The east tower now showed a 22,000 candlepower fixed, white light. The west light became a flashing 110,000 candlepower beacon. Simultaneously, a second-class siren was added on Dyer's Point in place of the steam locomotive whistle. The rationale for this change is not apparent, especially since the steam-powered signal had been deemed such a success only five years before.

Despite the many changes and improvements made at the station during the preceding ten years, shipwrecks continued to occur at an alarming rate around the entrance to Portland Harbor. Shortly after eight p.m., February 22, 1864, the transatlantic steamship *Bohemian*, inbound from Liverpool, struck Alden's Rock, two miles east-southeast of the end of the Cape. Late that afternoon, her master, Captain Robert Borland, had sighted the Cape lights as he searched for the pilot boat. But in the gathering darkness and thickening fog, he lost his bearings and his sense of distance from land.

Although the iron-hulled steamship had been proceeding at less than two knots when she hit, the jagged ledge tore a mighty hole in her undersides and she rapidly began taking on water. Captain Borland immediately turned the vessel toward shore and ordered full speed ahead, in an attempt to ground her before she went down. Within ten minutes, the rising waters flooded the en-gine room boilers and extinguished the fires. At this point, the crippled steamer was wallowing deeply, about a quarter-mile from shore and less than a mile north of the Cape station.

As soon as her headway had ceased, Captain Borland ordered the anchors let go and gave the word to abandon ship. Many of the passengers had been asleep

Cast-iron towers replaced the stone ones at the Cape Elizabeth station in 1874.

Above: Looking southwest, the east tower is in the foreground.

Below: The east tower is shown close-up looking east.

when the *Bohemian* plowed onto the rock and came stumbling out onto the decks, greatly confused and frightened. The call to leave the ship only heightened their anxieties. In the darkness, terror became panic for some, who swarmed the life-boats before they were ready for lowering. A davit pin on the No. 2 boat gave way under excessive strain, causing the boat to break loose. It splashed into the icy sea and swamped, drowning sixteen hapless souls, mostly women and children.

About 10:30 that night, the *Bohemian* sank in nearly five fathoms of water. The bulk of the ship lay along a long flat shelf of rock, with the bow and stern still several feet from the bottom. As she settled, several people milling about on the forecastle head were washed away. Others lost their lives when they jumped from the ship, thinking they would be picked up by one of the lifeboats, several of which reached shore only partially filled.

The final loss of life was nearly impossible to determine, since most of the survivors had scattered far and wide by the time the *Bohemian's* passenger lists were salvaged from the wreck. Ultimately, the toll was set at forty-two, mak-ing it one of Casco Bay's most deadly maritime disasters.

While the majority of the *Bohemian's* million-dollar dry goods cargo was later salvaged, the sodden remains of significant amounts of it — tea, crockery, broad-cloth, silks and threads, ribbons and buttons, furniture and silverware — washed free from the ship, onto beaches and into coves for miles along the coast. Much was finally retrieved, but some found its way into homes at the Cape and in surrounding communities.

In March 1865, the shattered hulk of an unknown bark washed up on the rocks near the station. Although much conjecture arose as to her identity, the answer was never forthcoming. The vessel had apparently gone ashore on Staples Point, just north of the lights, and had broken up during the night. No bodies were ever recovered.

On October 14, 1866, the schooner *Catherine Beals* sprang a leak coming in to Portland. Fearing for their lives, the crew left their ship near Ram Island Ledge, landing sometime later at the Cape. But the *Beals* did not sink immediately. Pushed by heavy seas, she drifted across the channel and grounded heavily near Trundy's Reef. Local residents spotted her the next morning, although before they could summon a tug to haul her off, the schooner had been battered to pieces.

Less than two years later the schooner *Kate Aubrey*, from Saco to Bangor in ballast, went ashore about a mile south of the lights, becoming a total wreck after only a few hours.

Trundy's Reef claimed another victim in August 1871 when the schooner *Sarah*, carrying 4,000 bushels of corn, stranded there during a heavy fog. The *Sarah* caught the ledge some distance from shore and her crew soon abandoned her. As the tide rose, however, the schooner worked herself shoreward until she lay completely out of water when the tide ebbed. In this vulnerable position she became a prime target for enterprising individuals, especially after the

Since 1902 the Cape Elizabeth Light towers have been white.

Above: The east light is shown shortly after the turn of the century.

Below: In 1924 the lantern cage and light atop the west tower were permanently dismantled.

Collection: Peter Dow Bachelder

The twelve-foot-square brick fog signal station associated with the Cape lights was constructed in 1886. It replaced an 1869 wooden structure which housed a boiler and twelve-inch steam locomotive whistle. The multiple horns, later operated by compressed air, were added in 1900.

vessel's owners allowed anyone to take whatever corn washed free from the wreck. Several days later, the *Sarah's* hull was sold at auction, commanding a price of thirty-five dollars.

The year 1872 was less than a month old when the schooner *Idaho*, coal laden from Port Johnson, New Jersey, sailed ashore in Broad Cove and bilged. Only a determined effort on the part of her salvors freed the vessel from a premature ending.

Final installation of the cast-iron towers in 1874 had left the Cape station in its best shape ever. Then during the winter of 1875-76, the Maine coast suffered under some of the most severe weather of the nineteenth century. A sleet storm in January was particularly devastating. At the keeper's house adjacent to the east tower, the howling gale broke the glass and sash bars in every window on its north side. When spring arrived, extensive repairs were required. The east dwelling got a new set of windows. The west residence had to be reshingled, have its windows reset and its sides re-clapboarded and painted.

In July 1880, the exteriors of both towers were painted white for better daytime visibility. Then two years later, the Lighthouse Board again announced it was doing away with the west light. The idea of its elimination created another tempest. Local storms of protest again reached all the way to Washington in strong opposition to "the injustices" threatened by the proposal. Public opinion prevailed and the whole idea was abandoned. One alteration did occur, however; both towers reverted to their former brown coloring.

During 1884, a first-order mineral-oil lamp was installed atop the east tower, lighted for the first time July 26. At the fog signal station in 1886, a brick water tank building twelve feet square was erected, although a recommendation for a duplicate fog signal was later turned down.

The keeper during these changes was Marcus A. Hanna, a former Civil War sergeant who had distinguished himself during the fighting at Port Hudson, Louisiana in July 1863, for which he had received the Congressional Medal of Honor. Hanna had come to Cape Elizabeth from Pemaquid Point Light in 1873, taking over his new duties just prior to the erection of the cast-iron towers. His career was highlighted by the last serious shipwreck near the lights — that of the two-masted schooner *Australia*, lost January 28, 1885. For his efforts in aiding the schooner's survivors, Hanna was again decorated by the government. He received the Life-Saving Service gold medal, the highest honor bestowed in such a situation.

The federal government had created the U.S. Life-Saving Service as an independent agency within the Treasury Department in 1878. Its charge was to organize the country's scattered and fragmented lifesaving network into a unified system providing professional assistance for shipwrecked mariners along Atlantic, Pacific, Gulf Coast, and Great Lakes shores. During the new agency's earliest years, Congress passed significant empowering legislation and

Placed in operation August 1, 1887, the Cape Elizabeth Lifesaving Station stood at the head of Dyer's Cove. The west tower of the Cape lights rises above the ridge (right) to the north of the station. The mast-like structure to the left of the flag is the drill pole, used by crews in their twice-a-week practices for breeches buoy rescues.

Collection: William B. Jordan, Jr.

Collection: Maine Historical Society

Crew members of the Cape Elizabeth Life-Saving station in front of their beach cart during a break from an October 1892 breeches buoy drill. L to R: Maurice Jordan, Joseph Staples, Sumner N. Dyer, Samuel D. Angell, Jesse Barker, Woodbury Pillsbury, and Station Keeper Captain Horace G. Trundy. Captain Trundy's dog Rover is in the foreground.

appropriated generous sums of money that enabled the service to build new stations and to update existing ones. In the process, it equipped each of them with functional rescue gear and employed station keepers who hired and trained crews of proficient, able-bodied surfmen to go to the aid of those in distress.

The first five life-saving stations in Maine were established during 1874, under the jurisdiction of the Revenue Marine Bureau. None of these was in Casco Bay, however — the closest being the Fletcher's Neck station at Biddeford Pool, ten miles southwest of Cape Elizabeth. In 1885, USLSS officials received funding for and authorized a station on Cape Elizabeth. The site they selected was at Dyer's Cove, below the Cape lights lofty location to the north, and adjacent to the fog signal house, to its south.

Built during the winter of 1886-87, the new facility went on active status August 1, 1887, coinciding with the start of the service's ten-month lifesaving season. Captain Horace G. Trundy was hired as station keeper and commanded an initial crew of six surfmen consisting of: Samuel D. Angell, Jesse Barker, Sumner N. Dyer, Maurice Jordan, Woodbury Pillsbury, and Joseph Staples.

In 1915, the duties and responsibilities of the Life-Saving Service were absorbed into the U.S. Coast Guard. Relegated to use as a boathouse and storage facility during the 1930's when the Coast Guard constructed larger quarters nearby, the original USLSS building was sold and moved away in 1952.

Refinements in station equipment at the Cape lights continued to be made at

Right: An aerial view of the twin towers at Cape Elizabeth Light taken by Don Johnson in the fall of 1994.

Don Johnson Photo

Architectural details of the keeper's house and the east tower at Cape Elizabeth Light.

frequent intervals after 1900. Immediately after the turn of the century, the big locomotive whistle first used so successfully more than thirty years before, was restored to duty. Months later, twin air horns were installed. In 1902, both towers were painted white once more and have remained this color since. Oil vapor lamps were installed in 1915 to provide better illumination.

The unwelcome winds of change blew again in January 1922 when word reached Portland that the west light would be de-commissioned The government had decided to do away with most twin-tower stations still in service. Other New England stations similarly affected included Matinicus Rock in Maine, and Baker's Island Lights and The Gurnet, both in Massachusetts.

Public protest was inevitable, but government surveys taken in advance had already satisfied those concerned there would be no great danger in employing only a single beacon. The change was a gradual one; in November 1923 both lights became fixed beacons, allowing for the dismantling of the west lantern. On May 9, 1924, its light went out for the last time. Six days later, the east light showed its new flash — a thirty second period consisting of six half-second flashes, with two and one-half seconds of darkness between each flash. Interspersed between each group of flashes were fifteen seconds of darkness.

To compensate for the removal of the west light, the east light's strength was increased to 500,000 candlepower on December 20, 1925, making it Maine's strongest lighthouse beacon.

During the decade of the 1960's, the U.S. Coast Guard essentially ceased its ongoing operations at and around Cape Elizabeth Light. In January 1964, it closed the lifeboat station adjacent to the lighthouse reservation. On March 1, 1966, Cape Elizabeth Light became automated, ending nearly 140 years of human habitation there.

In July 1970, the U.S. Post Office recognized the sesquicentennial celebration of Maine's statehood by issuing a six-cent commemorative stamp depicting the east tower of the Cape lights. Edward Hopper's famed painting "The Lighthouse at Two Lights" provided the scene used.

As early as June 1959, the General Services Administration began offering for sale the abandoned west lighthouse and 10.5 acres of surrounding land. Since then, the long-vacant tower has been owned by a succession of private parties, including actor Gary Merrill, who took possession for more than a decade beginning in 1971. Merrill presumably intended to transform the tower into his personal living quarters, although he never followed through on his objective.

Today, Cape Elizabeth Light displays the most powerful beacon on the entire New England coast. Regardless of the station's designation, local folks continue to refer to it as "Two Lights."

CHAPTER THREE

PORTLAND BREAKWATER LIGHT

O n November 22, 1831, a rapidly moving northeast storm devastated Portland Harbor, tearing up property and leaving a confused tangle of debris in its wake. Because the height of the storm's fury coincided with the time of normal high water, its violent winds pushed a monstrous tide into the harbor, which tore ships from their moorings, overflowed wharves and carried away several buildings. Within the inner harbor the rampaging waters also destroyed a portion of Vaughan's Bridge and undermined the banks of the Cumberland & Oxford Canal near its mouth, interrupting passage on both for several days. Damage in the harbor alone was estimated to exceed fifty thousand dollars.

Although the area's appearance quickly returned to normal, the storm's fury was to have a far more significant effect on the port in general than anyone then realized. Within months, many local residents were demanding protective measures to prevent further damage to their maritime interests. Echoes of these cries reached officials in Washington and prompted a directive dated November 1, 1832, from Secretary of War Lewis Cass to the Topographical Bureau calling for a survey of Portland Harbor "with a view to a plan and estimate of the cost of erecting a seawall or breakwater."

Within two weeks, Lieutenant Colonel John Anderson, of the Bureau's Engineers, had been dispatched to Portland from Weymouth, Massachusetts to conduct the called-for study. Accompanied only by a Lieutenant Poole, his map maker, Anderson tramped and rowed about the harbor, meticulously determining the exact position of each island, ledge and shoal. With craftsman like precision he sounded the nature and shape of the harbor bottom and the channels leading to it. From the data gathered, Anderson submitted a detailed proposal which reached Secretary Cass on October 19, 1833. The study recommended

An engraving from Elwell's *Portland and Vicinity* shows Portland Breakwater Light in 1875.

the erection of a rubble-stone breakwater along Stanford's Ledge, which marks the southern side of the inner harbor's entrance. According to the plan, the proposed structure would consist of seven sections and have a total length of more than 2,500 feet. Such construction would require nearly 46,000 cubic yards of rubble for the body of the work and another 3,500 cubic yards of ashlar stone for the top. Commenting on the availability of the stone, Anderson contended it "can be obtained in any quantity . . . within a short distance, from the shores of Little Hog (Diamond) Island, House Island, Bareze's (Peaks) Island, and on the shore south of the cape, south of the proposed work." The total cost of the effort, according to his best estimates, would come to $44,417.08. This would include "a pier and beacon on the outer end of the breakwater," which would be a necessity to mark the completed work

When presented for study and approval in the House of Representatives June 18, 1834, Lieutenant Colonel Anderson's survey also included plans for a breakwater on the so-called "middle-ground" in the harbor, between Stanford's Ledge and Fish Point, on the harbor's north side. This idea was later rejected. In fact, two years passed before final congressional approval occurred for any of the project, and a sum of $10,000 for the proposed Portland Breakwater was made available.

Construction efforts on the initial section, 401 yards long began in July 1836 under the watchful eye of Mr. Freeman Bradford, the resident engineer. With an average crew of thirty men employed, one-third of the rubble work was in place by early December. In a letter to his superior in Boston, Bradford explained that this section would be completed by the following June if his request for an additional $30,000 to finish it and begin the next four sections (a total of 287

Portland Breakwater Light in 1880.

1/2 more yards) could be met. Freeman's plea prompted another $25,000 during 1837 and a subsequent $26,366 the following year. With the application of these funds, the breakwater's foundation soon reached one-third of a mile out along the ledge, and Bradford happily reported in November 1837 "the portion of the breakwater already constructed has been found efficacious in keeping off the heavy swell that formerly swept over the ledge at high water."

But Portland Breakwater was never completed to the full extent of its original design. In 1838, and for several years thereafter, all requests for harbor improvements along the Atlantic coast were annually denied. After repeated attempts for additional local funds failed, work on the stone pier was officially suspended in 1852. At that point, roughly 1,800 linear feet of stonework had been laid, although a 683-foot section on the outer end lacked the final two coping courses, as did a 112-foot segment adjacent to the shore. Left for so many years in this partially finished condition, the unlighted breakwater evoked bitter complaints from unhappy mariners who viewed the structure more as a navigational hazard than anything else. But it was late 1854 before the U. S. Lighthouse Board gave the go-ahead for its engineers to lay out a proposal for a Portland Breakwater lighthouse. Conceived and drawn up in January 1855, the plan's details called for an octagonal tower with sloping, wooden sides to surmount two courses of ashlar stone set upon the breakwater's outer end. This would allow a sixth-order Fresnel lens to shine from twenty-five feet above high water. The plans were approved as submitted; construction was authorized on March 19, 1855 and was completed within four months.

During construction, W. A. Dyer accepted the appointment as the Breakwater Light's first keeper at an annual salary of $400. Dyer illuminated the fixed red light atop the tiny white tower for the first time August 1, 1855. When he stepped down in 1857, Dyer was succeeded by William L. Willard from neighboring Ferry Village.

The next decade witnessed a rather frequent succession of keepers at the light, including Benjamin F. Willard, 1860; Benjamin B. Walton, 1861; Len Strout, 1866; Paul McKenney, 1867.

Keeping the new light must have had its enjoyable moments, although there were certain offsetting problems. Because the unfinished portion of the breakwater barely showed above the high tide mark, commuting to and from the station, generally accomplished on foot, presented undue hazards. Many times angry waves slapped roughly against the uppermost stones driving sheets of spray high into the air, with the result that anything or anybody present got a thorough soaking. During the winter months, subfreezing temperatures sheathed the walls with a slick coating of ice. In this treacherous condition, it often forced a traversing keeper to crawl gingerly on his hands and knees its entire length.

Because the base of the wooden light tower stood only two feet above the normal high tide level it, too, was prone to frequent lashings during periods of unsettled weather. Dampness quickly worked into the dwelling below the light and government inspection teams were soon calling for new clapboards to cover the fast-becoming weather-beaten structure. Rust, always a problem around salt water, continually raised havoc with the cowl, or revolving metal hood above the lantern cage, which allowed proper ventilation for the oil-burning lamps. On nearly every annual check of station equipment, this cowl required either repair or replacement.

Toward the close of 1865, Colonel J. D. Graham of the Corps of Army Engineers examined the Portland Breakwater. He later submitted estimates for bringing the existing portion to "its proper level," and suggested it should "be extended at once 400 feet still further out" into the channel. To accomplish these projects Graham included detailed estimates totaling some $105,000 in additional costs.

Colonel Graham's proposal breezed through Congress without opposition, and under an act dated June 23, 1866, the entire amount prescribed was made available. Three months later, however, the whole project was thrown into a state of confusion so complex it could not be fully resolved for another year. The difficulty stemmed from the fact that Colonel Graham died before his plan could be carried out, leaving his successor, Brevet Brigadier General B. S. Alexander, heir to the operation. General Alexander had other ideas about the proposed extension, and one of his first actions was to conduct a new harbor survey himself.

Alexander's plan omitted many of Graham's concepts, and as a result its total expense came to only about $60,000, or little more than one-half the original appropriation. Its appearance prompted a statement from A. A. Humphreys, Chief of Engineers in Washington, who claimed his department was not willing without further information, to approve either plan until "a proper study of the questions involved" could be made, including a full series of current and tidal observations. Lieutenant Colonel George Thoms was selected to administrate the affair and he relieved Alexander. Thoms' ultimate report, submitted September 19, 1867, was accompanied by numerous maps and diagrams, and recommended that a minute survey of the harbor, to be carried out during October and November that same year by the U. S. Coast Survey, should later be considered in connection with the proposed works.

Thoms' detailed examination laid open to discussion further talks concerning general harbor improvements, including extensive dredging and widening of the harbor's main channels, for which several additional appropriations totaling nearly $150,000 were eventually made during the next decade.

Because there had been no disagreement by anyone concerning comple-

Arnold H. Valcour

Collection: Peter Dow Bachelder

Portland Breakwater Light station showed several additions and improvements shortly after the turn of the century. In 1902-03, the two-room keeper's dwelling received an addition of two rooms and an attic. In 1903, a 1,000-pound fog bell replaced the 400-pound one that had been installed six years earlier.

The iron steamship *Brooklyn* grounded on a submerged ledge not far from Portland Breakwater Light in April 1883. Nearly three months elapsed before she could be hauled free. The night she struck, the *Brooklyn* was heavily loaded with a general freight cargo for Liverpool, England that included 60,000 bushels of wheat; 93,000 pounds of bacon; 5,205 bags of flour; 4,975 bushels of peas; 1,143 barrels of apples; 423 cattle; and 240 sheep. Everything was saved.

Collection: The Mariners Museum, Newport News, Va.

A nineteenth century painting of Portland Harbor. Portland Breakwater Light appears on the right, with Fort Preble appearing in the middle ground to the left of the light. The Ottawa House on Cushing Island occupies the center of the painting, while a three-masted vessel makes its way into the inner harbor on the left.

tion of the unfinished capping of the existing stone work, during the summer of 1867 Colonel Thoms entered into contracts for this work with three Maine firms. Their operations commenced September 1, 1867, and were finished the following summer.

With so many phases of planning and construction under way at once, no actual work on the breakwater's extension could begin until September 1872. Yet within two months, workers had deposited 2,750 tons of stone at the site and had carried the job as far as possible prior to completion of the terminal pier. Quarrying and cutting the granite blocks required for this latter task resumed early the following spring, and the pier was finished in September 1873.

During this period the old wooden light tower continued to house the "Break-water Light," although an appropriation for a permanent tower was sought, since the wooden structure had by this time become "decayed and unfit for further service," in the words of the lighthouse inspectors.

On June 23, 1874, $6,000 was made available to erect a cast-iron tower, lined with brick. The following summer the wooden tower came down and was moved to the Lighthouse Board's First District reservation on Diamond Island, less than a mile away. A new tower, modeled on the Choragic Monument of Lysicrates, a nearly 2400-year-old Greek structure located in Athens, was placed upon an octagonal concrete base atop the recently completed pier-head. Slightly smaller than its wooden predecessor, the new tower stood thirteen feet, two and one-half inches high, and measured eleven feet, eight inches in diameter. Fashioned in Greek Revival style, it was considerably more elegant than it predecessor. Ornamenting its cylindrical shape were six iron Corinthian engaged columns and palmette, above which rested a circular lantern cage holding eight frames of quarter-inch plate glass.

The new Portland Breakwater Light went into operation late in June 1875, under the care of recently appointed keeper Stephen Hubbard, the seventh man to serve in that capacity.

Changes and improvements began affecting the new light almost immediately. On August 1, 1878, its fixed red beam became flashing red. A year later, a fifty-eight foot section of iron handrail went up along the breakwater at the tower's entrance, primarily as a safety measure. By 1886, it had been extended the entire 1,990 foot distance from tower to shore.

Over the years, several vessels have come to grief within sight of Portland Breakwater Light. Among these, one of the better known is the 3576-ton iron steamship *Brooklyn*, which plowed onto a submerged ledge near Fort Gorges one dark April night in 1883, while attempting to leave the harbor with a general freight cargo bound for Liverpool, England. The unyielding rock tore an extensive gash along the steamer's port side nearly amidships. The *Brooklyn's* mighty hulk soon became a familiar sight along the waterfront. since the combined task of unloading and refloating her consumed nearly three months and she lay another two months in dry dock undergoing temporary patching.

In March 1889, during Albus R. Angell's tenure at the station, a two-room wooden keeper's dwelling was constructed against the tower. Because of its eighteen by twenty foot dimensions, it overhung the breakwater on each side, although it survived in good shape for many years. Shortly after the turn of the century it received an addition of two more rooms and an attic. For general station protection, two hundred tons of riprap stone were placed about the end of the breakwater the next year.

Prior to 1897 a 400-pound electric fog bell had been used on the Stanford Ledge Buoy, slightly northeast of the light tower, but during that year it was removed and installed at the end of the breakwater. A few months later its operating machinery was taken out in favor of more more modern striking apparatus. By 1903 a 1000-pound bell had replaced the lighter one.

The year 1934 brought changes to Portland Breakwater Light which marked the beginning of its demise as a functional lighthouse. That year both it and the Spring Point Ledge Light were electrified. However, in the interests of economy, the government shifted control of the Breakwater Light to the tower at Spring Point via a submarine cable and the former became unattended.

When plans for the Todd-Bath Iron Shipbuilding Corporation to locate a shipbilding facility along the South Portland shoreline became a reality late in 1940, the useful days for the little light on Portland Breakwater were definitely numbered. As the year drew to a close, a veritable beehive of Todd-Bath men and machinery, under the able direction of Mr. William S. Newell, began transforming the long-deserted site of the old Cumberland Shipbuilding Company yards, just south of the breakwater, into a basin-type shipyard containing seven

Shipyard Society

World War II Liberty ships under construction at the West Yard of the South Portland Shipbuilding Corporation, June 19, 1942.

building berths. The new yard was a result of a contract between Todd-Bath and the British Purchasing Commission, which furnished funds for both the yard itself and for thirty ocean-type cargo carriers to help offset the staggering losses the British merchant fleet was suffering at the hands of German U-Boats.

So successful and rapid was the development of the Todd-Bath yard during the early months of 1941 that Chairman of the U. S. Maritime Commission Emory S. Land, then looking for an east coast site for an emergency shipyard, called upon Newell to supervise the building of another yard alongside the Todd-Bath facility for the purpose of building Liberty ships.

In this manner the so-called West Yard of the South Portland Shipbuilding Corporation came into being in the spring of 1941. Newell located the West Yard at Stanford's Point. To create additional space for the yard, he had thousands of cubic feet of earth hauled to the site. During the summer the shoreline around the point was pushed out into the harbor until the breakwater's length had been shortened by more than half. Situated directly over where the breakwater had stood, six ways or inclines were constructed upon which vessels could be built and launched.

Further changes to the surrounding land area occurred early in 1942, when the U. S. Navy, with an eye to putting in a giant repair dry dock, took possession of the section of shoreline adjacent to the south side of the breakwater. More fill was brought in and the shore line altered again until Portland Breakwater Light stood less than 100 feet from dry land. A dry-dock, in three sections, was actually towed to the spot, but the whole idea was later abandoned. The entire filled-in section was turned over to the Maritime Commission for its use.

At the completion of the British contract in November 1942, the Todd-Bath, or East Yard, together with the west area, then known as the South Portland Shipbuilding Corporation, were combined, and on April 1, 1943, the entire complex became the New England Shipbuilding Corporation.

United States involvement in the Second World War caused the Portland Breakwater Light Station to be shut down in June 1942. As it turned out, this was to be the last time the light would be actively used.

While the Breakwater Light had long been a familiar landmark among mariners, it achieved a different, farther-reaching level of recognition prior to its decommissioning.

In 1940, Edwin Turner, a South Portland High School student, designed and drew what the city officially adopted as its new municipal seal. A local ordinance from April that year declared:

> "The common seal...shall be engraved with a design consisting of the Portland Breakwater Light in the foreground, the water of the Harbor, with land in the background..."

During the 1980's, increasing concern for preserving the tiny lighthouse, known affectionately by local residents as "Bug Light," was registered with the Maine Historic Preservation Commission and it was placed on the National Register of Historic Places. As a result, private and public monies were raised for its restoration. Structural renovations and repainting, carried out in 1990, returned the Portland Breakwater Light to its best condition in recent memory.

Although its days of usefulness have long since vanished, anyone familiar with Portland's maritime past can hardly overlook the vital role this tiny light has played in the advancement of safety for the area's seafaring community.

Don Johnson

The cruise ship *Royal Viking Sun* passes Portland Breakwater Light in September of 1994. The light station is no longer in service and the dwelling house adjacent to the tower was removed in 1934.

CHAPTER FOUR

HALFWAY ROCK LIGHT

utside the island confines of Casco Bay with its countless snug coves and avenues of refuge stands Halfway Rock, a lonely, windswept patch of naked ledge, scarcely larger than a football field in size, looking strangely out of place several miles at sea. Treacherous ledges, jutting out several hundred yards north and southwest of the Rock are the only exceptions to the otherwise deep water surrounding this desolate spot. Webster Rock, rising to within eight feet of the surface, marks the culmination of the northern reef; while to the southwest a foreboding line of ragged rocks breaks the force of restless seas which predominate from southerly quadrants. This geologic formation allows a small but adequate landing site on the northern face, without which Halfway Rock would be all but inaccessible except in calm weather.

The name Halfway Rock was a logical choice for this spot since it very nearly bisects the twenty-mile distance separating Small Point and Cape Elizabeth, Casco Bay's eastern and western extremities. This isolated outpost lies along a time-worn route traveled by coasting vessels which have long used its jagged profile as a landmark. By the same token, its proximity to shipping has too often made it an object of dread and fear rather than an aid. Lost in the pages of time are many tales of hapless vessels, which during darkness and storm strayed too close to its cruel ledges and quickly perished. The Bath-built brig *Samuel* met such a fate in the late spring of 1835. In command of Captain George W. Small, the *Samuel* had been en route home to that Kennebec River port from Providence, when on June 19th, south of Cape Elizabeth, she encountered a heavy southeast gale. With twilight approaching, Captain Small became most anxious to steer his ship safely away from land, since during any southeast storm the entire Maine coast becomes a most inhospitable lee-shore.

Don Johnson
From the air, Halfway Rock Light rises majestically above the three acres of naked ledge on which it stands at the outer edge of Casco Bay.

Darkness enveloped the *Samuel* as she was sailing under a close-reefed foretopsail. During the evening the winds increased steadily and the brig raced ahead through angry mounting seas. Around ten o'clock that night the *Samuel* crashed heavily upon Halfway Rock. On impact, Captain Small and his steward crept forward to inspect the extent of damage to their vessel and possibly determine where they might be. The pair had inched out onto the jib boom when a giant breaking comber engulfed the ship and swept them both away. Terrified by the sudden loss of their companions, the remaining crewmen hesitated to try and save themselves; but the raging seas soon forced them into a hasty departure from the rapidly disintegrating vessel. Dropping from the lurching bow, they crawled out onto the sea-drenched ledge and clung together in fear the remainder of the night. Residents of Hope Island to the north spared the unlucky mariners any further hardships when they spied their distress signals the next morning and a volunteer crew brought the shipwrecked men to safety.

This disaster and others like it were instrumental in the makeup of an 1837 report concerning Halfway Rock submitted to Washington by Captain Joseph Smith of the U. S. Revenue Cutter Service when he stated:

> "In hazy or foggy weather, other rocks are sometimes mistaken for this and when this is the case, disaster is the probable consequence . . . Upon this rock I respectfully recommend the erection of a stone monument, and the cost of it I estimate at three thousand dollars."

Nevertheless, Captain Smith's request went unanswered for more than thirty years. Before action of any sort was even considered, another vessel went to pieces on Halfway Rock, this time in 1861, although its full story must forever remain unknown.

The first indication of disaster came on February 12th, 1861, when confused masses of wreckage began washing up on the southern tip of Jewell Island, more than three miles to the northwest of the rock, as well as on nearby Inner Green Island— deck planking, dunnage plank, knees and spars. Outside the islands, the waters fairly teemed with flotsam. A portion of the mystery was finally unveiled when a medicine chest with the single word *Boadicea* neatly printed on it was discovered among the tangle. Soon after, portions of a large vessel were found on and about Halfway Rock. Further investigation showed the wreckage came from the British bark *Boadicea*, which had cleared New Orleans on December 2, 1860, bound to Glasgow, Scotland. Because none of her crew was ever found, further particulars of the story could never be determined.

At long last, Captain Smith's almost forgotten plea had been given new impetus, although the erupting Civil War deterred any immediate action. On March 3, 1869, Congress authorized a lighthouse for Halfway Rock and appropriated $50,000 for its construction, setting August 1870 as a projected completion date. By June, final plans and estimates had been accepted by the Treasury Department and forwarded to the Lighthouse Board's office in Portland to be executed. Early in July the appropriation came through and the task of assembling a crew of men and providing them with working material began.

The light tower's design closely followed that adopted for use on the present

The dangers of landing from a small boat on Halfway Rock may be more fully appreciated in this view from a Coast Guard tender standing off the ledge.

Collection: The Mariners Museum, Newport News, Va.

tower at Minot's Ledge, outside Boston Harbor. This structure, completed in 1860, had been built to withstand a direct confrontation with the seas. Accordingly, the lowest portion of the proposed shaft would be a solid base of granite blocks, six feet high and dovetailed together on the sides, beds and tops. Rising from this foundation would be the tower itself, sixty feet high, twenty-two and one-half feet in diameter at the base and seventeen feet at the top.

Protective buildings for the workmen went up at the Rock in July, and the task of gouging out a level bed for the tower's foundation was begun. While this was in progress, massive granite blocks for the first courses were being quarried at nearby Chebeague Island, then cut and shaped at Fort Scammel in Portland Harbor.

The hurricane of September 8, 1869 pounded Halfway Rock heavily. During the storm, the schooner *Lydia* struck the Rock a glancing blow and barely managed to make nearby Bailey Island. Putting in at Mackerel Cove, the *Lydia* clearly showed the effects of her buffeting, having lost her mainsail, main boom, rudder, boats, chains and anchors. Below decks, her hold had completely filled with water.

Although the working quarters at the Rock had survived the storm, they had been weakened considerably and during another gale on October 4th they were completely destroyed. Despite the resulting delay, a work-suspension notice dated January 1, 1870 announced the foundation had been laid and stood ready to receive the tower walls.

Following the winter layoff, activity resumed in late spring, but because few landings could be made prior to June, little was accomplished until then. And yet Halfway Rock Light might well have been completed on schedule but for an unfortunate act passed by the 41st Congress June 12, 1870. Later termed a "shortsighted move," the law required that any appropriation for public works be expended during the fiscal year in which it was granted, or else be returned to the Treasury. Because of the lengthy delays occasioned by the weather, fiscal 1870 had ended before final purchases of material could be made. In mid-August with the job a few weeks from completion, all worked stopped. At this stage all the masonry was in place and material for the iron finish work had arrived on the Rock. With no alternative, workers covered the top of the tower with canvas and abandoned the site. Their tools and supplies were shipped back to Portland and stored.

On March 3, 1871, a $10,000 appropriation was made in Congress and the balance of funds again became available. Work resumed the first of July. Because all that remained was installation of the lantern assembly and miscellaneous iron finish work, the job was completed quickly and Halfway Rock Light went into operation August 15, 1871, manned by head keeper retired Captain John T. Sterling and his assistant, James Jones of Peaks Island.

Constructed of light gray granite, the finished tower reached sixty-six feet above the face of the rock below. A third-order Fresnel lens showing a fixed white light varied by red flashes once every minute beamed its friendly warning from seventy-six feet above the sea.

Human occupation of Halfway Rock almost immediately revealed a basic need at the new station. Each keeper's arrival and departure was made in a small boat, usually a rather risky undertaking since seas around the ledge were seldom calm. Surging waves and pounding surf often made putting to sea particularly difficult. To alleviate this problem a wooden, double-runnered boat-slip was bolted to the rocks. Sloping down across the face of the ledge to a point below the low tide mark, the rampway enabled the men to launch a dory with considerable momentum, thereby allowing them to concentrate more fully on pulling clear of the reef. At the same time the slip was laid down, a masonry boathouse, resembling a concrete igloo, was built near the top of the slip, just outside the tower doorway. The original slip lasted only ten years before deterioration from the elements caused its replacement. About 1890, a double slip was formed when a third rail was added to the existing pair.

As a result of their visits to Halfway Rock during the 1880's, the Lighthouse Board's inspecting teams decided that better quality, more powerful illumination was the top priority there. At least three times during the station's first twenty years, new revolving apparatus was ordered for the light. In January 1883, mineral-oil lamps replaced the original lard-oil ones. Three years later a vertical extension of the red flashing sequence "much improved the character-

Collection: Peter Dow Bachelder

Halfway Rock Light Station's efficiency was enhanced during its first twenty years of service with the 1887 addition of a 43-foot pyramidal bell tower connected to the lighthouse via a plank walkway and wooden railing; and with a two-story boathouse fastened directly to the tower the following year.

The elegant steamship *City of Bangor* (above) collided with her sister ship *City of Rockland* (below) off Halfway Rock on June 8, 1906.

istic of the light."

During the year 1887, a pyramidal, skeletal bell tower, forty-three feet high, took its place on the Rock, about eighty feet west of the lighthouse. Built of yellow pine timbers ten inches square and heavily bolted to the ledge, it supported a 1,000 pound bell, complete with striking machinery. A plank walkway with wooden railing connected the bell tower with the lighthouse. The newer structure received a severe test of strength the night of December 28 that same year. Monstrous seas flooded the ledges until water around the tower ran eight feet deep. Despite the vicious pounding, it stood firm.

The need for more and better living and storage facilities at the station prompted construction in 1888 of a two-story boathouse, having dimensions of eighteen by twenty-four feet. Fastened directly to the northern side of the lighthouse, its first story contained the station's dory and lifesaving equipment while also sheltering the upper end of the boat-slip. In the loft above, two dwelling rooms permitted additional living space for the light keepers. The new quarters were a welcome change from the cramped rooms within the confining tower, although the circular shaft had always been a place of welcome refuge during periods of extreme storminess.

A page in the station's log kept during the winter months of 1889 reveals the extent of one such lashing when even the tower's shelter hardly seemed adequate. On that miserable night during the height of a snarling easterly gale, one gargantuan wave rushed past the boathouse, reaching to the second-story eaves, fifteen feet above the ledge. The same wave swept away most of the plank walk and railing to the bell tower and bent the iron ladder at its base into the shape of a rainbow. Huge chunks of rock weighing several hundred tons were ripped and broken from the eastern end of the rock and carried nearly three hundred feet to the western side.

That same season the small outbuilding which had always sheltered the lantern's oil supply was destroyed. In its place a framed, shingled oil-house, eight feet square appeared the following summer beside the bell tower. Secured twenty feet above the rock with yellow pine timbers similar to those that held the fog bell, the oil-house gave Halfway Rock Light Station the general physical appearance it has assumed since.

When the old fog bell and machinery retired in 1905 in favor of a first-class trumpet, with a duplicate in reserve, many coasting captains must have felt some relief. Prior to the installation of the trumpet, government tests conducted around the rock concluded that whenever seas were breaking against the rocks, or anything more than a moderate breeze was blowing—which was a majority of the time—anyone upwind from the bell could hear nothing of its chime until he was nearly ashore on the Rock. Today's powerful horn emits two three-second blasts each minute during foggy weather and on a calm day or night can be heard from Cape Elizabeth, nearly ten miles away.

One of the more bizarre steamboat collisions along the Maine coast occurred

The loneliness at Halfway Rock continues today much as it has for more than a century.

within sight of Halfway Rock the night of June 8, 1906. In the wee hours of the morning, the Eastern Steamship Company's stately steamers *City of Bangor* and *City of Rockland* collided, narrowly avoiding what might have become a horrible tragedy. The big vessels, each on the Boston-Bangor route, had regularly crossed paths many times in the past without misfortune. That night patchy fog hung over the coast as Captain W. A. Roix of the east-bound *City of Rockland* made out his vessel's sister ship racing toward him through the mists about a half mile away. Swinging the wheel hard to starboard, Captain Roix sent the *Rockland* along at full speed to avoid the onrushing *Bangor*. But the *Bangor*, skippered by Captain E. W. Curtis, had swung hard to port, in a maneuver to get outside the *Rockland*. Locked on this deadly course, the burly steamships drove together, the *Bangor's* bow sinking deep into the *Rockland's* port quarter just aft of her big paddle wheel.

Damage to the *Rockland* was comparatively light despite her nearly fatal gash. Five staterooms had been crushed and about forty feet of her guard carried away. The *Bangor*, however, lost her stem down to the water line and immediately began taking on water. With the aid of the steamer *Calvin Austin*, summoned from Portland, the *Bangor* limped into that harbor, where repairs could be made. The *Rockland* continued her regular route to Bangor and later returned to Boston where she was patched up.

The *City of Rockland* remained with the Eastern Lines until 1923, when she went aground on the Kennebec River below Bath and had to be scrapped. The *City of Bangor* outlasted her sister by ten years before she sank at her wharf in East Boston and was abandoned.

More recent improvements at Halfway Rock include a major facelifting in 1960, which brought a new boathouse and more modern quarters for the resident Coast Guard keepers, as well as a helicopter landing apron the following year. The latter, a forty-foot square concrete slab intended for emergency use such as illness or accident, was laid in a depression blasted as much as six feet into the solid rock by a U. S. Army demolition team. Its appearance added one more link the station personnel could enjoy with the mainland. Electricity and telephone kept them in constant touch with the world about them. Once every week a tender from South Portland allowed a rotation of duty among the three-man crew, while landing needed goods and supplies.

All this was a far cry from the station's earliest days, when "going home" to a keeper usually meant a lonely, often treacherous, eleven-mile row into Portland, attended by what ever whims of weather might intervene. And yet, over the years life on the Rock itself changed comparatively little. The long hours of solitude always existed, punctuated by the necessary chores involved in performing the exacting maintenance of all station equipment to insure good running order.

Don Johnson

Their maintenance tasks completed, two Coast Guardsmen leave Halfway Rock by small boat. This photograph was taken in the 1960's.

Fierce weather periodically continues to pound Halfway Rock, as it did during an early-October storm in 1962. Winds and water tore at the station with a savage fury seldom seen anywhere. Twenty-foot waves literally engulfed both the tower and the outbuildings. The receding waters revealed a broken boat launching ramp, a twisted shambles of catwalks, railings and porches, and only half the helicopter landing pad.

Today, however, scenes like this are only haunting memories for those who were once stationed there. With the assistance of Coast Guard helicopters, the automation of Halfway Rock Light Station was carried out during January of 1976. What remains is the solitary granite tower with its nearby landing site, which allows easy access for the maintenance crews who make periodic visits.

CHAPTER FIVE

Spring Point Ledge Light

nbound fishing boats chug noisily by, surrounded by scores of swooping gulls. In the distance the island ferry hurries past, seemingly oblivious to the world around it. On occasion a monstrous tanker, its bowels swimming with raw oil from half a world away, slips noiselessly up the channel and carefully noses in to its berth, prodded on by tireless harbor tugs. Forts Gorges and Scammel, cold and silent sentinels of another generation, anchor the nearest islands while partially masking their more distant counterparts. With its massive iron foundation forcibly immersed in these chilly harbor waters, Spring Point Ledge Light looks mutely out upon this close-up view of Portland's marine scene as it has since its establishment in 1897 adjacent to the main shipping channel.

The installation of Portland Breakwater Light in 1855 had convinced the newly-formed U. S. Lighthouse Board that it had at last adequately marked Portland's inner harbor approaches. Scarcely a year had passed, however, before the local citizenry had called the Board's attention to one significant omission in its deployment of aids—the lack of any marker at Spring Point Ledge. Located opposite Fort Preble, almost one mile southeast of the Breakwater Light, this partially submerged ledge pushes seaward several hundred feet, ending abruptly in bold water dangerously close to the main channel. Over the years it became fairly common for an errant vessel to hang up here. In most cases the stranded ship managed to work herself free, assisted by the rising tide. Occasionally, though, one would be less fortunate, as was the schooner *Nancy*, a lime coaster which came ashore September 7, 1832. The shock of impact shattered the schooner's hull and set fire to her cargo. Most of her sails and rigging were eventually saved, but the vessel ended up a total loss when she burned to the water's edge.

After due consideration of the public request, the government anchored a huge spar buoy to the outer end of Spring Point Ledge. Its effectiveness was questionable at best. The strandings continued at frequent intervals, as stories of the vessels *Mazatlan, Seguin, Solomon Poole, Smith Tuttle* and others can attest. But perhaps the most spectacular wreck here occurred during the savage equinoctial gale March 20-21, 1876, which claimed dozens of vessels and lives along the New England coast. Local newspapers remarked how waves within the harbor swept over waterfront wharves and that "a boat could sail along Commercial Street in two feet of water."

During the early hours of March 21 the fine new bark *Harriet S. Jackson*, running in ballast, piled heavily against Spring Point Ledge. With the great storm howling near its height, visibility had been so reduced by rain and fog that the *Jackson*, attempting to run for cover, rammed ashore without any previous inkling of danger. Overpowered by relentless breakers, the helpless vessel jolted across the rocks, completely at the mercy of the rising tide. As dawn broke slowly that morning, the *Jackson's* crew stood peering directly into Fort Preble, only a few yards ahead of them. When the tide began to ebb, the bark canted over on her starboard side so close to the southeast corner of the fort that the entire crew walked to safety simply by laying a plank from the vessel's taffrail to the earthworks ashore.

Word of the *Harriet S. Jackson's* fate flashed to Portland, where many parties were anxious to save the vessel. At successive intervals during the day, no less than four tugs steamed out around the breakwater to examine her. Each in turn tried its best to pull the 393-ton bark free, but without success. That afternoon Captain Bacon, the *Jackson's* skipper, rode the tug *Warren* out to view the wreck. The tide was then low and the vessel lay far up on the rocks. The water that had been in her hold had drained completely out, making it an easy job for Bacon to thoroughly inspect his ship. Much of the bark's starboard side had been badly stove in. The copper sheathing protecting her undersides had been neatly stripped clean when the vessel dragged across the ledge, and several ugly gouges scored her hull.

Despite what he saw, Captain Bacon spoke confidently that he could rescue his ship. That same afternoon, he and his crew began removing the ballast from deep within her battered hulk. They lashed empty hogsheads along her keel and throughout the hold. Bacon hoped that if the *Jackson* could be pulled free, the barrels would keep her afloat long enough for him to get her into dry dock. On March 23, two harbor tugs hitched onto the bark prior to high water. They strained for more than an hour, but could only bring her back to an upright position. A second attempt two days later combined the efforts of three tugs and a revenue cutter. After much urging, the big vessel slowly scraped her way

Opposite: Cross-section of Spring Point Ledge Light.

Collection: Peter Dow Bachelder

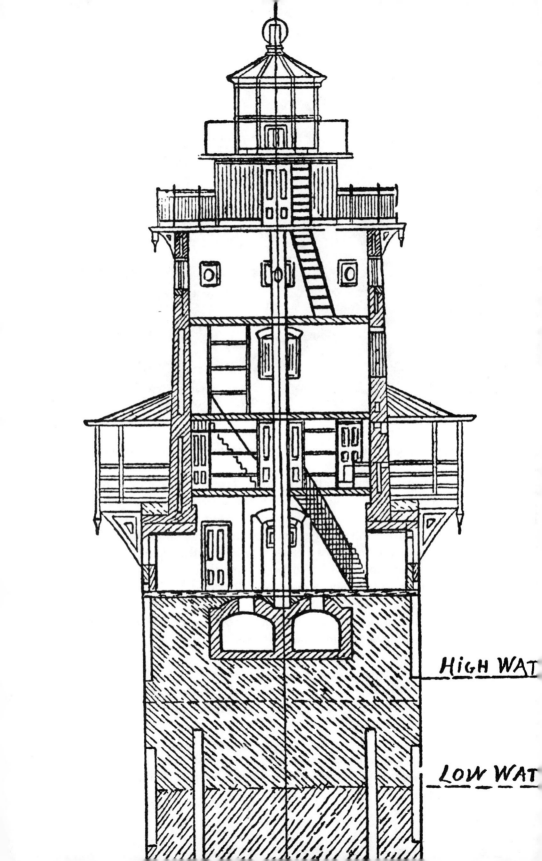

HIGH WAT

LOW WAT

Collection: Howard Reiche

Spring Point Ledge Light as depicted by an unknown nineteenth century artist.

stern first into deeper water. In this crippled condition, she was hauled up the harbor to the Dyer yard in Knightville for repairs. The *Harriet S. Jackson* later returned to service and continued in regular use until lost off Cape Cod in 1898.

Considerable attention was again focused on Spring Point Ledge in 1891 when the seven steamship companies then serving Portland presented the Lighthouse Board a resume complete with figures showing that their vessels annually carried more than a half-million persons past this point. In the interest of further safety, it asked that a fog bell and light be erected at the ledge as soon as possible. The Board presented a formal request to Congress for this construction, estimating it could be accomplished for $45,000. Although the initial request was denied, similar ones were faithfully repeated each year until 1895, when on March 2nd that year Congress authorized a contract calling for the establishment of a fifth-order light and a fog signal station not to exceed $45,000 in cost, and set aside $20,000 to begin the job. Fifteen months later it made available the remaining $25,000.

From plans accepted by government engineers, the proposed Spring Point Ledge lighthouse would consist of a circular foundation pier supporting a three-story circular dwelling, a veranda with boat davits, a circular parapet and an octagonal lantern cage. The foundation pier was actually a cast-iron cylinder, twenty-five feet in diameter, forty feet high and open at both ends. Composed of forty-eight sections, the cylinder would be bolted to the ledge in fourteen feet of water and the lower portion of it filled with concrete. The upper section, to be divided by numerous straight brick walls, would house various compartments for the storage of oil, fuel and other supplies.

Thomas Dwyer of New York City received the contract to erect and equip the tower. After the preliminary steps necessary to level the foundation rock, work of laying the foundation began the first week of August 1896. With a full-time diver employed, initial assembly moved ahead rapidly until Sunday, September 6, when a blustery southeast storm dumped five inches of rain on the Portland area. Wind-wracked seas tossed into the bay and up the harbor caused an unusually heavy undertow. When workmen returned to the ledge on Monday, they found many of the 1¼-inch iron plates forming the foundation pier badly twisted and broken. Everything they had accomplished to that point had to be undone and the job started over from the beginning. Damage estimates to the tower alone ran as high as $5,000, to say nothing of the time lost or the added expense for labor and materials.

Because the iron work had been contracted for from the Allentown Rolling Mills in Pennsylvania, three weeks went by before replacement sections arrived in Portland, and another three days passed before they could be inspected and reach the ledge.

In an effort to regain the original schedule, which called for the tower's completion by the end of December, Dwyer placed a large gang at work night and day bolting the foundation together. On October 25th the tower showed above water for the first time. Then early in November all work stopped again. Government inspectors condemned the whole job because of the type of ce-

The United States Coast Guard bark *Eagle* abreast of Spring Point Ledge Light on a visit to Portland harbor.
Don Johnson

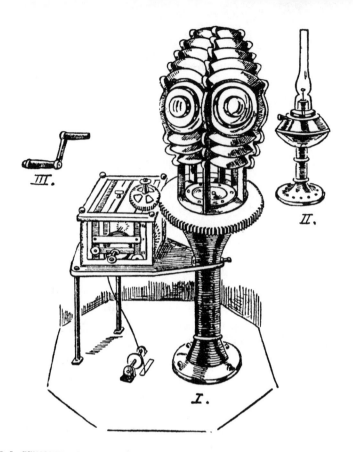

NO. I.—REVOLVING CLOCK. NO. II.—LAMP FOR REVOLVING CLOCK. NO.III.—CLOCK-KEY.

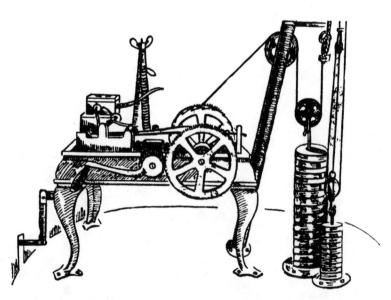

BELL STRIKING MACHINERY AND CLOCK WEIGHTS.

ment being used to fill the foundation. Arguments ensued and charges and countercharges flew back and forth. The inspectors demanded that the work be rebuilt a second time; while the contractors, who had previously stated publicly that the entire job had become a losing proposition, claimed to have suffered from the inspectors' incompetency. Another three weeks elapsed before the impasse was resolved to everyone's liking and work resumed once more. Dwyer's work was deemed satisfactory and he was allowed to continue without interruption.

With winter's onset, occasional work stoppages due to contrary weather conditions prevented a rapid completion of the work. The lantern cage went up early in February 1897, whereupon workmen shifted to minor interior finish work. On March 17 the tower received a coat of paint and was finished except for installation of the kerosene lantern, which did not arrive until April 2.

As soon as the formalities of advertising the new station had been met and the selection of keepers was announced, Spring Point Ledge Light went into active service May 24, 1897. William A. Lane, appointed March 15, became head keeper.

Within the tower, the keeper's quarters had been provided with all the available comforts and conveniences. The first floor served as a cellar, divided into several coal closets and a deep alcove to house tools and equipment. The floor above, reached by ascending a circular iron staircase connecting each level, was considered the kitchen. The third floor was home and office for the head keeper. Now completely dark since the station was automated in 1934, this room was formerly brightened by four rectangular windows which afforded commanding views of the surrounding harbor.

Above, on the fourth level, were the assistant or second keeper's quarters, equally as spacious as those of his superior. From here, an iron ladder led to the watch room above, where the clock weight and bell striking machinery were located. On the balcony outside hung the big fog bell, immovable in an iron swing riveted to a platform. During foggy weather the bell was rung with an iron hammer by means of a rather intricate system. From the center of the hammer handle, an iron pipe ran back into a loop coming through a slit in the watch room which connected with the winding machinery inside. This in turn was connected to 800 pounds of weights which provided the bell's ringing power. A bell cord ran downward to the cellar through a central pillar in the tower. To keep the bell ringing continuously, it was necessary to rewind the cord once each hour.

Above the watch room stood the lantern room, reached by another iron ladder. Here, housed in an octagonal cage was the lantern with its heavy, bevelled-glass lens. Its light, once furnished by kerosene via a tall, brass lamp, has been

Opposite: An 1897 artist's drawing reveals Spring Point Ledge Light's clock, lamp and bell striking machinery.   *Collection: Peter Dow Bachelder*

Collection: Peter Dow Bachelder

Two views of Spring Point Ledge Light: (above) from Fort Preble showing Fort Gorges at the far left; and (below) an inbound tug passes the tower and ledge at low water.

Collection: Peter Dow Bachelder

powered electrically since 1934.

Today's 200,000 candlepower white flash beams forth once every five seconds through a seven-degree sector, marking the fairway of the main channel at the harbor's entrance. Outside this narrow arc the flash is red, 4,500 candlepower strong. Inbound vessels guiding on the white flash can safely steer by it until they reach the safety of the inner harbor.

Although it had been contemplated for more than a century, the granite breakwater connecting Spring Point Ledge Light with the mainland was not completed until 1951. Proposals for such a structure had been discussed at the close of World War I as a means of sheltering the old Cumberland Shipbuilding Company's yard near Cushing's Point. The idea was revived once about 1930 and again in 1941 when construction of the Todd-Bath Shipyard on the Cumberland yard site was announced, although no definite action resulted.

In July 1946, a document approved by the 79th Congress gave the U. S. Army Corps of Engineers authority to supervise the building of a 900-foot granite breakwater along the ledge; however, nearly three years passed before any funds were forthcoming. In March 1949, the U. S. House of Representatives allotted $255,000 to begin the project.

Design plans called for the finished structure to stand fifteen feet above mean low water and be composed entirely of three-and five-ton granite chunks. Its seaward wall would slope about thirty degrees to the horizontal; on the harbor side, the incline would be greater.

Construction of a granite breakwater along Spring Point Ledge was begun in mid-1950 and completed exactly a year and a day later.

Guy Gannett Publishing Company

Semitrailer trucks belonging to the Chase Transfer Company of Portland brought the granite, 15 tons per load, to Spring Point from quarries at Biddeford and Wells. A crane capable of lifting thirty tons plucked the pieces from the flat beds and transferred them to the seawall. Initial work began June 6, 1950, and exactly a year and a day later the completed the breakwater, comprising 50,000 tons of stone, had been laid up at a total cost of nearly $200,000.

During its annual spruce-up of navigation aids, a civilian Coast Guard crew spent the better part of May 1957 sandblasting the thirty-foot section of Spring Point Ledge's light tower above its main deck, the first time this had been done in its sixty-year existence. The cylinder was then painted with a white vinyl paint, found to be highly resistant to weathering.

Spring Point Ledge Light's importance today is sometimes difficult to understand. The decision to eliminate Cushing Cove, between Fort Preble and the Portland Breakwater, and the subsequent emergence of two shipyards and an oil pipeline terminal almost adjacent to Spring Point, have greatly altered the appearance of the surrounding land until the very presence of this lighthouse almost seems unnecessary. At the same time, those who must count on its friendly light to guide them safely up the channel realize that its role continues to be extremely vital to all harbor shipping.

Opposite: Aerial view of the 900-foot granite breakwater connecting Spring Point Ledge Light with the mainland.   *U.S. Coast Guard*

CHAPTER SIX

RAM ISLAND LEDGE LIGHT

Brisk southeast winds and occasional spatters of rain lent an uncomfortable air to the departure of the Allan Line steamer *Californian* from Portland, February 24, 1900. Leaving her berth at the Grand Trunk Wharf shortly before midnight, the sturdy 400-foot steamship gathered speed slowly as she churned down the harbor on her regular transatlantic crossing to Liverpool, England. An hour later the *Californian* lay hard aground on Ram Island Ledge, at the northern side of the harbor's entrance.

In a simple case of misjudgment, Captain John France, the *Californian's* master, had allowed his ship to stray slightly from her normal course. Before he discovered his error, the *Californian* struck Ram Island Ledge bows on, grating along heavily until she came to a halt, cradled tightly in a slight hollow in the massive reef.

What might have been a needless tragedy was neatly averted with the successful rescue of the *Californian's* twenty-one passengers and $300,000 general freight cargo. The steamer herself was pulled free six weeks later, her undersides badly damaged. Patched up and taken to Boston, the vessel later returned to regular service.

The near loss of the steamship *Californian* forced serious thinking about the need for further navigational aids at the entrance to Portland Harbor. Her spectacular stranding focused public attention on hazardous Ram Island Ledge, a jagged, wave-torn finger of rock one-quarter of a mile long, which marks the northern entrance into Portland's outer harbor. Running off in a southwesterly direction from nearby Ram Island, its mere presence has made it a spot greatly feared by mariners, especially during thick or inclement weather.

As early as 1855 Ram Island Ledge was marked by an iron spindle placed near its southern end, although it proved useful solely as a daytime aid. In 1873 a fifty-foot-high wooden tripod replaced the spindle. Clumsy as it was this contraption made a definite improvement, except that its exposed position left it vulnerable to an almost constant buffeting from the open ocean, and at least three times it washed completely away.

Such a device was in use the night the *Californian* went aground, a fact that caused serious conjecture about what might happen there in the future without a more substantial aid to mark the ledge. Within days the talk became strong demands for a lighthouse, demands which led to an eventual $166,000 congressional appropriation for that very purpose. A portion of the money was provided June 28, 1902. Before the job could be put out for bids, however, government engineers decided not to allow any work to start until the following spring. As unfortunate as this delay might have seemed, little could have been accomplished sooner, since the rock on which the tower was to stand lay submerged two-thirds of the time. Even during the summer months when seas around the ledge were relatively calm, work could be carried on only a few hours at a time. The actual construction would have to begin in the spring, as soon as longer periods of more tranquil weather allowed. Yet all this was of little consequence to the men aboard two vessels lost on Ram Island Ledge that fall.

On September 22, 1902, the British three-masted schooner *Glenrosa* ended her sailing days at the ledge. Deeply laden with 850 tons of culm coal for the S. D. Warren Company in Westbrook, the *Glenrosa* was inbound for Portland in a dense fog. Off Cape Elizabeth her skipper, Captain Finley, had picked up the sound of the big fog horn at Portland Head. Steering by this, he was confi-

An aerial view of Ram Island Ledge Light from the collection of Don Johnson.

The steamship *Californian*, which ran aground on Ram Island Ledge in 1900, brought to the public's attention the need for a lighthouse at that treacherous location.

dent he had his vessel squarely in the middle of the main channel leading up the harbor. Then without any warning the *Glenrosa* came to a sudden, quivering stop against Ram Island Ledge. Overwhelmed, her crew momentarily stood dumfounded, unable to react. After sailing so close to their destination, they suddenly realized they didn't know exactly where they were. While they were wondering the schooner gave a lurch, pulled herself free and slid back into deeper water. The unexpected movement brought the sailors to their senses and they rushed frantically for the anchors. As they fumbled with the chains, the *Glenrosa* started ahead once more. Striking the rocks again, she wedged herself tightly into a crevice where she held firmly.

Because only a slight sea was running when the *Glenrosa* grounded, her crew stayed aboard safely until daylight. With the first gray streaks of dawn, they put off in a lifeboat and landed on Ram Island. When the fog burned off later in the day, they rowed into Portland.

Anxious to get the *Glenrosa* off the rocks, Captain Finley wasted no time making arrangements with Captain Phil Doyen, a local wrecker, for stripping his vessel. But since the following day was Sunday, Doyen refused to touch the schooner until Monday. The delay provided a golden opportunity for the area's private salvors. All day Sunday, scores of tiny craft hovered about the wreck, carting off whatever seemed to their owners' liking. The looters worked on the principle that the schooner had been abandoned and was therefore the property of anyone, despite a solemn promise from the *Glenrosa's* owner to make an example of anyone caught at the site.

Doyen's postponement of working the wreck resulted in further difficulties at the site. Sunday's weather was ideal, but during the early hours of Monday morning, rough seas built up. All that day the wreckers found it impossible to bring a lighter close enough to the ship to do any work. By the time heavy equipment moved in on Tuesday, most of the schooner's fittings and even a small portion of her cargo had disappeared.

During the rest of the week, the lighter *Atlas* made occasional visits to the *Glenrosa* and saved a few spars, a portion of her sails and some rigging. On October 7 an auction was held in Portland, comprised of all the wreckage that had been brought ashore. Even the schooner's hull went up for bids and was sold as she lay, still on the rocks. The gentleman who purchased it must have felt he had gotten quite a deal when the sale price of four dollars was handed down; although as much of a good thing as it may have seemed then, he soon found out he had gotten very little for his money. The next morning reports reached town that the *Glenrosa's* hulk had broken up, and only a small section of her bow remained on the rocks.

The Chebeague Island stone sloop *M. M. Hamilton* carried granite blocks for the construction of Ram Island Ledge Light from Central Wharf in Portland to the building site.   *Collection: Peter Dow Bachelder*

Less than three months later, the ninety-five foot fishing schooner *Cora & Lillian* met a fate practically identical to that which the *Glenrosa* had suffered. But in the case of the *Cora & Lillian*, work to save her began immediately. Two days later, though, a southeast storm set in, and that night giant waves completely battered in the vessel's sides until she broke apart and sank.

The loss of the schooners *Glenrosa* and *Cora & Lillian* served only to shorten the patience of those who had been waiting for a lighthouse on Ram Island Ledge. What further proof they may have needed to assure a light's existence there had been provided, and they were most anxious that concrete steps be taken without further delays.

Actually, on September 15, 1902, the U. S. Lighthouse Board had formally authorized construction of the light station "by direct hire of labor and the purchase of materials of the lowest bidder." Under the Board's direction, the task of coordinating and administrating this undertaking continued throughout the winter. On March 10, 1903, title to Ram Island Ledge was obtained from two Cape Elizabeth families for $500. By the end of the month, a contract had been written with the Bodwell Granite Company of Rockland to provide stones for constructing the light tower. These would be cut from the company's Wharf Quarry at Vinalhaven and freighted to Central Wharf in Portland. After carefully being numbered to indicate their position in the structure, the big blocks would be ferried to the ledge as needed by the big-bellied Chebeague stone sloops *M. M. Hamilton* and *Yankee Girl*.

Because wintry weather lasted unusually late into the spring of 1903, work at the ledge itself did not begin until May 1st. The initial task consisted of cutting down and leveling the foundation rock to three feet above mean low water. For this, a crew of forty was hired and placed under the supervision of Mr. James Howard of Portland, with Captain Alfred Hamilton of Chebeague Island acting as foreman in charge at the ledge. Temporary quarters had been erected in April on nearby Ram Island where the men could stay while not on the job.

As contrary as conditions had been prior to the commencement of work at the rock, the opposite was true during the following weeks. An extended spell of fine weather, with a resulting lack of winds and dangerous seas, produced two months of remarkably steady work, during which area 28 feet in diameter was cleared and leveled. On June 30th, the rock was ready to receive the first stones.

A special derrick and a hoisting engine were set up at the ledge and a 100-foot platform was then built to protect both men and masonry. On July 9, the first granite blocks arrived. These were placed upon the foundation in circular courses, each consisting of twenty stones weighing nearly four tons apiece. The steam tug *Ocean View*, normally a pilot boat for the English steamers entering Portland, was hired to serve as a stores vessel, and stood by while the men worked, in case the wind should freshen and make evacuation necessary. But fine weather held, and within a week two courses were in place. Tranquil con-

Cutting and shaping of the Cyclopean blocks of granite at the Bodwell Granite Company on Vinalhaven Island. A total of 699 stones was taken from the quarry, then and cut and shaped to form the Ram Island Ledge lighthouse. The Vinalhaven sloop *Harvester* transported the granite to Portland. On each trip, she carried twenty massive blocks, each weighing nearly four tons. Before being ferried to the construction site, each stone was numbered to indicate its position on the tower.

Collection: Peter Dow Bachelder

During the summer of 1903, workmen at Ram Island Ledge erected 320 four-ton granite blocks and backed them with concrete.

ditions the rest of the summer aided in speeding work along rapidly, and by the time operations were suspended for the year on September 30, sixteen full courses had been laid, bringing the tower to a height of 32 feet. Within the structure, concrete backing had been put in, two cisterns had been brought up to their full height, their manhole frames set and the covers put on.

All activity did not stop that fall. As the weather permitted, additional stones were measured for and cut in Vinalhaven; the interior iron work and a landing ladder were completed in a Boston machine shop, interior woodwork was fashioned in Portland, while a third-order Fresnel lens was ordered from Paris.

April 1904 brought the resumption of outside work. With a crew of twenty-five men employed, the job progressed smoothly, and by early July the final stones were in place. A total of 699 light gray granite blocks had been utilized, costing $33,679.40.

As soon as the tower itself had been completed, interior finish work commenced. The first task consisted of placing enameled brickwork around the interior walls. While this was in progress, the sixteen-foot steel lantern cage and iron parapet took shape atop the newly-laid lantern floor; whereupon workmen topped the cage with a two-foot brass ball and lightning rod, bringing the lighthouse to its full height of more than ninety feet.

The tower's 26,000 pound lantern, constructed in Atlanta, Georgia, arrived in Portland by rail the last week of September. Made from tobin bronze, it had been packed in wooden crates aboard two railroad cars. Mr. O. C. Luther, a government master mechanic, came from Boston to supervise its assembly and installation, which was completed by mid-October.

During early August, inspecting Lighthouse Board officials had decided that a large iron pier, suitable as a landing site, should be constructed upon the ledge. This was in addition to the original plans; but because of the light's dangerous position during rough weather, they felt it a necessity to insure the safety of both men and material during their transfer to and from the station. At the Board's recommendation, the proposed structure measured seventy feet long, twenty feet wide and stood eighteen feet above the ledge.

Money for its construction was available from already appropriated funds, unused in building the tower, and the job began at once. During the next few weeks, holes for the pier's uprights were hand-drilled five feet into·the solid rock, large enough to hold four-inch pillars set in cement.   December 1st had been set as a tentative date for placing Ram Island Ledge Light Station in operation, in time for the various steamship lines' winter schedules. But delays in the shipping of materials denied this, and work was suspended a second time January 23, 1905.

Although not in the original plans for Ram Island Ledge Light, an iron landing pier, 70 feet long, 20 feet wide, and 18 feet high, was built during 1904-05, to facilitate the transfer of men and material to and from the station during rough weather.

Collection: Peter Dow Bachelder

As it has since 1905, Ram Island Ledge Light stands its lonely vigil at the northern side of the entrance to Portland Harbor. The landing pier was removed after the station was automated.

The work slowdown proved quite fortunate for the four-man crew of the two-masted schooner *Leona*, out of Rockport, Maine. Early Wednesday, January 11, the *Leona*, in the capable hands of Captain L. S. Whitten, had sailed from Rockland for Boston with a capacity cargo of lime. Her trip progressed quietly until evening when the schooner came abreast of Seguin Light, off the mouth of the Kennebec River. Here a stiffening southeasterly breeze and a few lazy snow flakes foretold nasty weather. Captain Whitten, wary of any adverse conditions with his ticklish cargo, decided to head for Portland and ride out the impending storm. The *Leona* was a stout ship, but at thirty-four years old, she was one of the older coasters then in the downeast trade. Besides, Captain Whitten knew that the open sea during a southeast storm was no place for any lime coaster, new or old.

The *Leona* passed Halfway Rock after midnight, where Captain Whitten noted extremely sharp visibility despite scud-filled skies and ever roughening seas. Within the hour the storm struck in full force, blotting out everything with its wind-whipped fury. By this time, the four sailors had brought their schooner close to the harbor's entrance. With safety nearly at hand, they found themselves sailing blindly into a swirling gray-white gloom. For what they could see, they might as well have been a thousand miles at sea; it would have been a lot safer.

Captain Whitten believed the best hope for their survival rested on whether or not he could get a bearing from the fog signal on Portland Head. Ordinarily this would have been an easy matter, but because the wind was from the wrong quarter, neither he nor his men could hear the whistle except during infrequent lulls in the gale. Even then it seemed many miles away.

While the *Leona's* crew was straining to hear the horn, the schooner drifted rapidly from her intended course. Minutes later she hit a ledge off the eastern side of Ram Island and keeled over.

Reacting with alarm, her four crew members sprang into action. First mate Walter Harriman sounded the schooner's pumps and found the vessel still tight, although he could only guess how much longer she would maintain this condition. Mountainous waves broke cleanly over the ship, allowing tons of green water to cascade wildly across her decks. With lime in her holds, the *Leona* lay like an ignited powder keg. Each man knew the results if and when water reached the cargo. Water and lime combine violently; the lime gives off terrific amounts of heat, capable of starting a fire within seconds.

His fears heightened by the imminent danger, Captain Whitten gave the order to abandon ship. With the sails still slatting noisily above them, the sailors struggled quietly as they put their tiny lifeboat over the schooner's stern. As soon as it reached the water they dropped into it one at a time and cast off.

Ahead of them lay the almost impossible task of getting away from the ship, and to accomplish this meant rowing directly into the teeth of the storm. But the determined sailors would not be denied their single chance for safety. Pulling until every fiber in their arms and shoulders burned, they slowly inched their way clear. Forced to battle every wave just to keep afloat, the four had no idea which way to go. With blind hope they thrashed about, trying to keep the frail boat headed up into the wind. At every turn the drenching spray and icy needles of snow cut through them, robbing their strength and gnawing at their desire.

The *Leona's* crew had left their crippled schooner at approximately three o'clock in the morning. For three long, tortuous hours they fought the raging storm until it seemed they were approaching the very limits of human endurance. Shortly before dawn each man began to despair of any further hope. As a last resort, Captain Whitten lit one of the distress flares he had carried with him off the schooner. At successive intervals he lit others until they were all gone. He had little idea who might be awake to see any of them, or whether such signals would even be seen at all through the storm. But in his mind it seemed better to try anything and hope, than to do nothing and freeze.

In the little wooden shack on Ram Island that housed the crew still employed at the lighthouse, a group of chilly workers huddled together listening to the storm howling around them. Occasionally peering outside, one of them glimpsed the faint glow from a distress rocket through the predawn darkness.

Shaking off his drowsiness he spoke briefly to the others, and hurried out into the snow. The rest followed him, carefully making their way to a bluff overlooking the open ocean where their comrade had seen the glow. For a time they just stood there hunched over, unable to see anything except the blinding snow and angry surf. Several minutes had passed when the *Leona's* lifeboat appeared near the shore still containing the pitiful forms of four men struggling feebly to stay afloat. By shouting and waving frantically, the workmen made it understood there was a landing place on the back side of the island.

At this point the men in the lifeboat were driving themselves to their utmost to make any progress at all. After another half-hour's effort they managed to land the boat in a rocky cove on the island's western shore. There to meet them, the construction gang rushed the shivering quartet up to their shack where they made things as comfortable for them as possible. In a few hours, the men had recovered enough from their exposure to be taken to Portland where they could tell their harrowing story to the authorities.

That forenoon, water seeped into the lime aboard the *Leona* and the schooner exploded in flames. By the time help arrived to battle the blaze, the vessel was too far gone to save. The next day, no trace of her remained.

Finish work at Ram Island Ledge Light had sufficiently advanced during the spring of 1905 so that the 8,000 candlepower kerosene lantern atop the seventy-foot granite shaft was first illuminated officially an hour before sunset April 10. The original lighting system was operated by two counterweights hung on long heavy chains. Their controlled drop turned the glass reflectors in the lantern cage to give the desired light characteristics, two white flashes every six seconds. A hand-operated winch hoisted the weights back to the top of the tower and kept the mechanism running properly.

William C. Tapley received appointment as the first head keeper, a position he held until February 1929. Over the years it became customary to have a crew of three keepers assigned to the station. Each stood a two-week tour of duty, working a twelve-hour shift each day. On completion of this he received one week's shore leave.

The idea of the new light's relative isolation despite its closeness to the mainland made it a popular tourist attraction, especially during the summer months of its earlier years. With nearly an acre of ledge out of water at low tide, the area soon became a mecca for adventuresome picnickers and curiosity seekers. In pleasant weather whole families often showed up. Many spread their tablecloths upon the rocks and enjoyed an open-air lunch. After the meal, a leisurely inspection of the big stone tower and light station capped a most enjoyable stay. Often fishing parties also took advantage of the spot. Tasty cunners weighing two and three pounds apiece could be caught from the rocks with relatively little difficulty. Occasionally other more enterprising individuals used the craggy ledges to rake sea moss. One man bragged to Mr. Tapley that he earned as much as $500 a summer this way.

The changeover to electricity at Ram Island Ledge did not come until late in 1958. In November that year, the Coast Guard announced that the conversion from kerosene had been assigned to a crew from its South Portland base, add-

As a solitary gull glides above the water, Ram Island Ledge Light is almost obscured by a July fog bank.

ing that plans for the station's automation would be carried out as soon as the job was completed. Underwater power cables for a new 20,000 candlepower beacon were laid between the ledge and Portland Head where light and fog horn controls had been installed. On January 14, 1959, Ram Island Ledge Light became an unattended station.

The effectiveness of this lonely outpost can be readily measured by the fact that no notable shipwrecks have occurred near it since its inception in 1905. Today the tower carries on its lonely vigil, vacant except for occasional main-

CHAPTER SEVEN

THE PORTLAND LIGHTSHIPS

ell prior to the mid-nineteenth century, Portland Harbor had begun to receive considerable attention with respect to the establishment of appropriate aids to navigation there. Until then however, its two offshore approaches continued to go unmarked. Inbound vessels from the south and west customarily worked in through the southern entrance, which brought them close to Cape Elizabeth. Those from down-east came in past Halfway Rock, a barren outcropping ten miles east of Cape Elizabeth. As early as 1811, Captain Lemuel Moody of Portland had conducted a survey to pinpoint the significant dangers along these routes by using the stone monument at the southern end of the Cape as a reference point. He later published a chart of Portland Harbor and listed Alden's Rock, Bulwark Shoal, and Taylor's Reef, among others, as obstructions he felt should be marked. These deadly pinnacles lurked only a few feet beneath the ocean's surface and often came awash during periods of heavy weather.

Many of the hazards noted by Moody lay along West Cod Ledge, a six-mile barrier of broken ground south and east of Cape Elizabeth, as well as along a parallel shoal extending from the Cape to Ram Island Ledge. Deep, natural channels through these submerged reefs afforded easy passageway during clear weather and calm seas. But finding a safe route here during foggy or stormy conditions was a matter of considerable risk at best. And yet, a quarter of a century elapsed following Moody's survey before any of these danger points was marked for the mariners' benefit.

Alden's Rock was the first of the southerly obstructions to be so identified. In 1835, a forty-five-foot wooden spar buoy was anchored nearby. The cedar spar, finished in red for better visibility, rose twenty feet above the ocean's surface and held a twelve-foot staff with attached red flag. On a clear day, the flag was discernible for six miles or more. In 1855, the buoy was replaced by a black iron bell-boat showing the words ALDEN'S ROCK in white letters on each side and supporting a 500-pound bell that sounded by wave action.

During 1846, other spars were positioned over Broad Cove Rock and at the seaward end of Trundy's Reef, along the Cape shore. Within the next decade, several other nearby trouble spots, including Old Anthony Rock and Taylor's Reef, were similarly marked.

Along the eastern approach, a spar buoy had been set over Bulwark Shoal in 1846 and an iron spindle buoy driven into the southern tip of Ram Island Ledge in 1855. By 1873, a fifty-foot wooden tripod had replaced the Ram Island spindle. Two years previously, a lighthouse had been established on Halfway Rock, and by the close of the century, plans for a similar structure were in the process of being formulated for Ram Island Ledge.

The final significant Casco Bay offshore aid was established in 1903, although its real beginning dates from the preceding decade. For several years, area mariners had been suggesting that a lightship off Portland would provide the necessary focal point to allow easier, safer passage to and from their harbor. In 1897, they persuaded Senator William P. Frye of Lewiston to present their case in Washington

On January 5, 1898, Senator Frye introduced a bill during the second session of the 55th Congress which called for "construction of a light ship, with fog signal, to be located near Cape Elizabeth, Maine, at a cost not to exceed seventy thousand dollars." It was referred to the Senate's Committee on Commerce for study. Reported on favorably later in the month, it survived a vote of the full Senate and moved along to the Committee on Interstate and Foreign Commerce in the House of Representatives. The proposed act was then tabled until the next congressional session, which convened that fall.

By the time deliberations on the measure commenced, House committee members had been virtually showered with petitions and letters on its behalf. Topping the list of proponents were management officials from several of the various steamship lines serving Portland, who had circulated petitions in support of the proposed lightship. Executives from the Portland, the Maine, and the International steamship companies actively worked to enlist the backing of those with local maritime sympathies.

Their efforts garnered long lists of signatures from leading local merchants and ship owners. Even the Mayor of Portland signed one. Many other organizations made known their feelings individually. Standard Oil Company of New York, mindful of its own business interests which passed through the local port, wrote a strong letter of support, as did the local Merchants' Exchange and Board of Trade, the Maine State Board of Trade, the Grand Trunk Railway System, and others.

The concerns of all involved were greatly relieved and their hopes much encouraged when the U. S House concurred with the Senate's earlier action, and on March 3, 1899, the bill to construct a lightship "to be located near Cape Elizabeth" was enacted.

Later in the year, the nine-member U. S. Lighthouse Board drew up plans and specifications for the new lightship, advertised the job, and put it out for bids. Thirty-eight contractors showed enough interest to request proposal forms and specifications booklets; however, when the March 1, 1900 date arrived for opening and reviewing the job bids, only four had been submitted. At $77,837.00, the Petersburg Virginia Iron Works was the low bidder, although their figure exceeded by nearly eight thousand dollars the amount Congress had made available. Faced with the problem of finding additional funds, the Board went to Secretary of the Treasury L. J. Gage, who in turn asked the House of Representatives for an additional $20,000. Gage's letter in support of his request stated:

> "In view of the increase in the cost of labor and material since the (original) estimate was prepared as to the cost of this vessel, and in view of the fact that, from additional information since received, it has been necessary to furnish her with towing machinery, and several other details the better to fit her for the exposed and exceedingly dangerous position she is to occupy, and to better fit her for the job she is to do, the Board asks that the proper measures may be taken to have $20,000 more appropriated for the building of this vessel; that the appropriation be made at the earliest date practicable; and that the amount when appropriated be made immediately available."

Congress found no objection to the request, and on June 6, 1900 appropriated the full amount. In the meantime, the Lighthouse Board had worked out a contractual agreement with the Petersburg firm:

> "to furnish all the materials and labor necessary to completely construct and deliver (one light vessel) to the Light House Inspector at the Buoy Depot at Little Diamond Island, Portland Harbor, Maine, within twelve calendar months from the date of the contract (May 16, 1900) for the sum of $77,837.00."

Petersburg Iron Works had been established in 1854. A property of H. T. Morrison & Company, experienced manufacturers of steam engines, dredges, and tug boats, the company had enjoyed a history which included satisfactory completion of other government contracts. There was every reason to believe that Petersburg would fulfill its obligation within the prescribed time and deliver the lightship to everyone's liking. Such was not to be the case.

National Archives

(Above) Built in Virginia, the *Cape Elizabeth* lies tied up at the Petersburg Iron Works wharf on January 7, 1903. (Below) The *Cape Elizabeth* stands on her station, 5.3 miles east-southeast of Cape Elizabeth on March 18, 1903.

National Archives

Work at Petersburg began on schedule and progressed as planned until fall. In October, though, some Lighthouse Board members decided they preferred a different type windlass (the apparatus for hoisting the anchor) installed. In place of the steam-powered model originally intended, they requested an automatic riding one which would allow the anchor cable to be paid out or taken in instinctively as the lightship rose or fell with the seas. Such a rig relieved undue strain on the cable and made it less likely a vessel would go adrift during a storm.

By itself, such a minor modification should have had only a minimal effect on the overall job completion timetable; however, a further problem arose. The manufacturers of the automatic windlass, with whom Petersburg had subcontracted, declared it would take six months before they could deliver one. As it turned out, this incident was just the first in a series of setbacks that would completely alter the intended work schedule. In fact, when the May 16, 1901 delivery date arrived, the lightship was less than sixty percent finished.

Despite this and several similar problems, Petersburg had reached a point late in 1901 where it had begun installing the lightship's outward machinery, one of the last steps prior to putting the vessel in the water. That time arrived Tuesday, February 11, 1902. In the presence of several hundred people, the lightship *Cape Elizabeth*, as she had been named, was christened with a bottle of wine by Mrs. W. M. Mays, wife of the port warden, and slipped from her ways on Swan's Island into the Appomattox River.

Expecting the previous August that delivery of the lightship to Portland was then imminent, the Lighthouse Board had selected a partial crew for the vessel. John E. Ladd, then mate aboard the Pollock Rip (Massachusetts) lightship, was chosen captain. Thomas H. Ingersoll of Portland would be his mate. Also appointed the same date were John B. Weatherbee of Massachusetts as engineer, and Edward L. Eaton as fireman. Weatherbee was then assistant engineer on the Nantucket New South Shoals lightship, while Eaton was a fireman on the lighthouse tender *Geranium*. A cook, two firemen, and five sailors would be selected later — much later as it turned out. Already some nine months behind schedule, Petersburg would still need another year almost to the day before it could fully complete its job and send the lightship to Portland.

Finish work delays — including floods, washouts, in-house strikes, and differences of opinion between Petersburg and the government's inspectors — continued well into 1902. Although communications between Petersburg and the government became increasingly prolific, their relations grew strained and deteriorated to the point where the Virginia firm threatened court action to win money it felt was long overdue.

Simultaneously, discussions came to a head early in 1902, both in Washington and in Portland, on another subject — the exact location of the new lightship's station. The original bill of authorization had not been specific. Its

Relief No. 53 stood in for *Cape Elizabeth* while she underwent repairs and modfications during 1906 and 1907.

intent had been aimed toward the construction of the vessel. The only reference to location had been "near Cape Elizabeth."

Portland skippers favored a position close to the Cape, although they disagreed whether the spot should be southeast or southwest of there. From their perspective, the deep water pilots using the harbor wanted a location near the whistling buoy south of Halfway Rock. This position, some ten miles southeast of Cape Elizabeth, would essentially mark the harbor's eastern approach and be much closer to their transatlantic route. In the end, however, the Lighthouse Board chose a site about five miles southeast of the Cape. It based its choice on a report made in 1897 by Thomas N. Perry, its Naval Secretary.

Perry had carefully studied both harbor approaches and had recommended a spot which "would be accessible from all seaward directions, and from which vessels could take a departure and steer in a straight, safe course through the ledges to the harbor," adding that such a location "would remove the present dangers and difficulties in a great degree."

By the end of 1902, the difficulties between Petersburg and the government had been resolved — at least temporarily. Final fitting out of the lightship had then progressed to the point where, early in 1903, the 495-ton vessel was pronounced ready for her sea trials. Leaving Smith Point the morning of February 9th, she dropped down river and arrived at Newport News late in the afternoon. The following morning, after taking on ten tons of bituminous coal , she proceeded to sea off Cape Henry for a sixteen-mile run. By evening, she was back in Newport News, tied up at the Smith & McCoy Shipyard and set to head north.

Unfavorable sailing conditions detained the new lightship in Virginia for more than a week. Ultimately, she reached Cape Elizabeth at 9:30 a.m., February 23, and within a half-hour had tied up at the Little Diamond Island Buoy Depot in Portland Harbor. Over the next several days the vessel received her stores and anchors. Her crew came aboard and attended to the myriad last-minute details necessary to make her shipshape prior to her arrival on station. The evening of March 6, the lightship steamed across the harbor to the Grand Trunk wharf, where she spent the night.

At eight o'clock the next morning, in company with the buoy tender *Lilac*, the spanking new Cape Elizabeth lightship sailed out of the harbor to a position 5.3 miles east-southeast of the east tower of the Cape Elizabeth lights, or more precisely, at 43° 31.6' north latitude and 70° 05.5' west longitude. Moored in 150 feet of water, she was held in place by a 5,000-pound mushroom anchor attached to 135 fathoms of chain.

Physically speaking, *Cape Elizabeth* was a stout vessel. Built of oak framing and pine planking, her keel, stem, and stern posts were fashioned from the best seacoast white oak available. Her timbers were also white oak placed twenty-two inches apart on centers. Five-inch seasoned yellow pine formed her planking, which was copper-sheathed to a line fourteen feet above her keel amidships, sixteen feet forward and fifteen feet aft, a total of 5,200 square feet.

As such, *Cape Elizabeth* was the last U. S. lightship ordered built entirely from wood. Metal-hulled ships had begun replacing wooden vessels more than twenty years previously. The changeover had been extremely slow, however, because marine architects had long felt that a metal hull was unable to absorb the constant buffeting the sea gave a vessel at anchor. Metal, they also argued, allowed the growth of impeding marine life much more rapidly than wood, or even copper-sheathed planking. Furthermore, they believed that in warm weather a metal-hulled boat would heat up excessively, causing the hull to sweat and the insides to become too dank and unpleasant to be habitable.

Above the waterline, the lightship had been designed with a long forecastle deck and deck house, where the crew's quarters, the fog signal machinery, and upper engine room were located. She had been fitted with two spruce trysail masts, one just aft of each steel lantern mast. Fully rigged, she carried three sails.

The vessel's power came from a coal-burning, steam engine. Eighteen steel tanks provided an aggregate capacity of 8,700 gallons of water to two cylindri-

National Archives

In 1913, the U.S. Bureau of Lighthouses changed the name of the Cape Elizabeth light-ship to *Portland*, feeling the new name was more clearly associated with the vessel's purpose, to mark the outer entrance to Portland Harbor.

cal boilers which produced one hundred pounds of working pressure. Her steam-powered fog signal sounded from a chime whistle twelve inches in diameter and operated by clockwork. In case of whistle failure, a 1,000-pound bell stood as backup equipment. Steam also provided heat for the vessel. There were radiators in the cabin, each stateroom, two in the forecastle, and one in the windlass room.

On station, *Cape Elizabeth* made a colorful sight. Painted a deep red for greater daytime visibility, she showed the words CAPE ELIZABETH in bold white letters along both sides of her hull, together with the number "74" fore and aft of the name. The Lighthouse Board had assigned No. 74 to *Cape Elizabeth* at the time her specifications were drawn up in 1899. It had begun numbering its light-vessels back in 1867 as a means of keeping better track of them. The original sequence of numbers was determined, not as one might think, according to each vessel's age, but by its geographic location — in a north to-south progression. At that time, all light-vessels then in service were stationed either in Atlantic or Gulf coastal waters. The northernmost ship, the Nantucket New South Shoals light-vessel, became No. 1, and each successive number was assigned to the vessel next further south. In later years, each time the Board used the next highest number when a new ship was commissioned, it created a system that assumed an increasingly chronological meaning.

For nighttime identification, No. 74 showed two fixed white lights from the mastheads of her twin sixty-foot masts. Her original lanterns burned oil, although they were replaced in 1911 by acetylene ones.

During No. 74's first weeks in service, the vessel drew widespread praise from many, including the Surveyor of the Port of Portland, former Civil War General Joshua L. Chamberlain. It seemed at last that all who had worked so hard to bring the lightship to Maine waters could rightfully be pleased.

In early June, however, a petition written on Eastern Steamship letterhead reached Captain George A. Merriam, Lighthouse Inspector for the First District, headquartered in Portland. Signed by twelve of Eastern's own masters and pilots who regularly sailed in and out of Portland, the request asked that the lightship's fog signal be changed from a three-second to a ten-second blast. Eastern's skippers claimed they couldn't hear the present signal until they were less than a mile from it. Even within that range they felt the three-second whistle was too short to allow them to accurately determine No. 74's position. By way of comparison, they mentioned the fact that the Boston lightship's horn could be heard for six miles and suggested the Board install a similar one aboard the *Cape Elizabeth.*

Although the Lighthouse Board strongly defended its reasoning for selecting the signal then in use, it replaced the whistle that summer and again a second time three years later. Between these changes, it lengthened the characteristic of the newer horn from three to five seconds.

Following this and other minor modifications to the lightship in 1903, the

Following the completion of her days as the Portland lightship in 1931, No. 74 lived out her usefulness as the Hen & Chickens lightship off Buzzards Bay, Massachusetts.

Lighthouse Board arranged to bring No. 74 into port once every two years for a complete overhaul. On these occasions, she was usually replaced by a relief lightship specifically designated for this task. Most often, it was one assigned to Second District headquarters, out of Boston, since *Cape Elizabeth* was the only lightvessel serving within what was then the First District, comprising Maine and New Hampshire waters. During No. 74's years of service, at least five different relief ships stood in for her.

Prior to the appointed time for her biennial going-over in 1911, the U.S. Congress had abolished the Lighthouse Board. Feeling its nine-man administrative head had become too cumbersome, the legislative body had replaced it with the Bureau of Lighthouses, in charge of one person. The Bureau was retained within the Department of Commerce, where it had been transferred in 1903 from the Treasury Department. George R. Putnam was selected to head the new agency.

Under Putnam's guidance, No. 74 came off station in September 1911 and was taken to Tompkinsville, New York, where in addition to her general overhaul, she received new acetylene gas lanterns in place of her oil-fired ones.

Before beginning her duty as Portland, No. 90 served as the Hedge Fence lightship off Martha's Vineyard, Massachusetts.

Lightship No. 90 served as the Portland lightship from 1931 until 1952, although she was taken off station from January 1942 until September 1945, to join the Seventh District Atlantic Coastal Defense Unit off Key West, Florida.

During her stay at the General Depot there, a small fire started in the drum room early Christmas morning. Quickly extinguished, the blaze nevertheless caused an estimated $1,300 damage.

In June 1913, the Lighthouse Bureau recommended changing No. 74's name from *Cape Elizabeth* to *Portland*. The proposed action was in keeping with a broader directive seeking to shorten the names of all existing lightships. The Bureau indicated the name *Cape Elizabeth*, besides being longer, wasn't really appropriate, inasmuch as the lightship wasn't marking any shoal or reef off Cape Elizabeth; rather, it was acting as a guide to the entrance to Portland Harbor. In late-September, it formally approved the name change and authorized arrangements to have the ship repainted the next time she docked for repairs, ostensibly that fall. The paint job was completed October 28th.

Unfortunately, in the rush to make the change, nobody in Portland bothered to read the original directive thoroughly enough to notice it also specified that all the numbers on each vessel's hull were to be removed at the time the name was changed. It was the last week of March 1914 before this oversight came to light. The numerals were quickly removed before the end of the month.

Over the next several years, the Portland lightship served her station in routine fashion. Her biennial visits landside continued, primarily for cleaning and repairing. Intermediary changes and improvements were usually performed while the ship was on station, such as installation of her first radio transmitter in 1917. Each successive visit ashore, however, witnessed an increasing need for repairs, and hence spiraling maintenance costs.

For instance, dry-docking and repairing costs in 1918, which included retubing one of her boilers, came to slightly more than $2,000. In August 1924, docking/repair costs included retubing the boilers again. This time, the bill amounted to more than $8,300. Just four months later, another $4,800 was required to provide, among other things, a radio fog signal and an oil-engine generator. Electric lights were considered at this juncture but the idea was turned down.

A pattern was becoming evident. With her advancing age, the wooden-hulled lightship had become an increasingly larger liability, yet was spending less and less time at her post. During the period 1918-1922, relief vessel No. 86 had been replacing *Portland* whenever she came off station, often standing in for six weeks or more at a time.

In retrospect, No. 74's fate already had been determined by the early 1920's. During her 1924 dry-docking, her boilers were retubed and routine hull repairs were made — nothing more. In January 1925, authorization for a 500-watt radio fog signal and communications transmitter was given, although the installation was delayed until the vessel's biennial overhaul in mid-1926. A conversion to electricity was again discussed but was curtly refused via an official statement which read in part: "...it is not the intention...to equip the ship with electric lights at this time." When the new transmitter eventually was installed, it was only 200-watts strong, not the 500-watts promised.

Two years later, the matter of the change to electric lighting was discussed a third time, but once again was rejected. In July 1930, No. 74 sailed to Boston for sorely-needed repairs — no longer simply preventive maintenance, rather a furtherance of the evermore expensive restoration necessary to keep the aged vessel in operating shape. Simultaneous with her dry-docking, word came down from Acting Commissioner of Lighthouses, H. D. King, that the Lighthouse Bureau had decided to permanently replace No. 74 with No. 90, which had been acting as her relief since 1924. Instead of being retired, No. 74 would be assigned a less-exposed position in the Second District.

Portland's new home would be located at the entrance to Buzzard's Bay, Massachusetts, where the relatively ancient No. 42, more than fifty years old, had been serving. No. 74 would take her predecessor's name, *Hen & Chickens*, so-called because the duty station lay adjacent to a dangerous reef of rocks that resembled a mother hen and her trailing brood.

Following her departure from Maine waters in March 1931, No. 74 entered the final stage of her long and proud career, beginning a period of decline that saw her rapidly outlive her usefulness. In March 1934, when the government retired the vessel and put her up for sale by sealed bid, her worth was placed at $100.

Meanwhile, No. 90 had quietly assumed her duties as the new Portland lightship on March 19, 1931. She was a product of the Fore River Shipbuilding Company of Quincy, Massachusetts in 1908. A flush-deck, iron-hulled vessel with a flat bottom, she proved much more seaworthy than her earlier counterpart. Her shapely malleable iron hull represented the most advanced design construction for a vessel intended to withstand the constant pounding to which lightships were subjected.

Prior to taking the name *Portland,* No. 90 had in turn spent time on the Hedge Fence Shoal (1908-1913) and Vineyard Sound (1913-1915) stations, both off Martha's Vineyard, Massachusetts. In 1915, she began sixteen years of service as a relief vessel, initially standing in for ships in the Second District — eventually including First District *Portland.* And while she symbolized a higher plane of technological know-how in lightship design and structure, in other ways she sorely needed improvement and updating — not the emergency, patch-up type, but the kind that would raise her overall efficiency and effectiveness.

The first such upgrading occurred during late-summer 1932 when a diaphone fog signal, operated by compressed air, was installed in place of her steam whistle. Slightly more than a year later, bids were sought to convert the ship from coal- to oil-burning. This latter step was a significant one, since during the lightship's coal-fired days, a tender had to make the fifteen-mile round trip from Portland every month to consume a tedious two-day bunkering task. By contrast, oil refueling would be necessary only once a year — a simple, one-hour job that could await the most favorable conditions. The conversion was accomplished at the Bethlehem Shipbuilding Corporation yard in East Boston late in 1934, during the vessel's annual overhaul. The following year, a radio-telephone gave the lightship instant ship-to-shore communication.

The Presidential Reorganization Act of 1939, an attempt to streamline and consolidate existing government agencies, abolished the Bureau of Lighthouses. Its responsibilities were transferred to the jurisdiction of the U. S. Coast Guard, resulting in the return of administrative control of aids to navigation to the Treasury Department, where it had initially been placed 150 years earlier.

One of the changes effected by the Coast Guard during its restructuring of the Bureau of Lighthouses was a renumbering of existing lightships. Employing a combination of letters and numbers, the agency labeled each vessel with a three-digit designator prefixed by the letters WAL (and later WLV). Under this new system, *Portland* was officially known as WAL-514, although through the remainder of her career most local mariners commonly called her No. 90.

Although standing duty off Cape Elizabeth provided long stretches of relative peace and quiet for the newer *Portland,* there were tense moments, as well. On January 24, 1936, the four-masted schooner *Alvena,* running light from Portland on a return trip to Jacksonville, Florida, took a sudden strong gust of northwesterly wind just as she was passing the lightship. The schooner's stern swung about and struck the lightship near her port bow. The light-vessel's spare anchor came clattering down on the *Alvena's* quarterdeck, splintering a sec-

The third Portland lightship, No. 111, was built in Bath, Maine in 1926. She saw service along the New Jersey coast and off New York before returning to Maine to serve as *Portland* from 1952 until 1969.

tion of her railing and damaging the adjacent planking. After heaving to off Halfway Rock, the *Alvena* limped back into Portland for repairs. Damage to the *Portland* was negligible.

The decade of the 1940's brought American involvement in World War II. The Portland lightship, in company with the Boston and Pollock Rip lightvessels, was withdrawn from her station January 14, 1942 and taken to a position off Key West, Florida. Armed with several guns, she became a unit in defense of the Atlantic coast. Her place off Portland was taken by a lighted buoy. During 1944, she returned to New England and was stationed in Chelsea, Massachusetts as a relief ship. Following V. J. Day in September 1945, No. 90 was back at her customary post five miles off the Cape.

Although Portland Harbor had been without the services of a lightship for more than three and one-half years, the local scene had enjoyed the services of Lightship No. 112, the *Nantucket*. Throughout the war, the Navy operated her as a surveillance and examination vessel, anchored just outside the submarine net at the harbor's entrance, to identify and clear incoming and outgoing marine traffic.

In three successive years during the late-1940's, the Portland lightship or her relief vessel survived as many serious brushes with disaster. Near the height of the great Cape Elizabeth gale of March 3, 1947, *Portland* first lost her big mushroom anchor together with sixty fathoms of chain, then bent her crankshaft before being driven more than four miles off station. With the cruel ledges of the Cape shore looming ever nearer, she was saved from almost certain calamity when her spare anchor finally caught and held the crippled ship from being unmercifully tossed ashore. She was later taken in tow by the Coast Guard cutter *Cowslip*.

U.S. Coast Guard

During World War II, Lightship No. 114 was stationed off Diamond Shoals, North Carolina, one of the most treacherous locations along the Atlantic Coast. Prior to that she had served as *Fire Island*, *Relief* and *Pollock Rip*.

The following March, the Canadian tanker *Rincon Hills* struck the lightship a glancing blow along her starboard side, about twenty feet from her bow. The impact punched a five-foot dent in the lightship's hull. Although the concussion dislodged a few small fittings, the diminutive ship survived otherwise unharmed. Then on October 8, 1949, during No. 90's annual overhaul, her relief, No. 106, was rammed by a 180-foot patrol boat attached to the South Portland Naval Reserve Training Center. The relief vessel received a sixteen-foot vertical gash from her weather deck to a point nearly a foot below the waterline. Luckily, the point of impact occurred at one of the lightship's ribs, where two steel plates overlapped and had been joined together by rivets. Later inspection of the damage elicited the opinion that had the collision occurred as little as a few inches either way from where it did, the cutter's prow would have driven straight through the lightship, slicing her in two. As it was, the two riveted plates were sprung several inches apart.

Number 106's crew, most of whom had been taken by complete surprise, were unhurt, although some had been thrown several feet across the deck. As the vessel began to take on water, the sailors hurriedly covered the submerged portion of the gash with a mattress, shored by planking, thus averting any danger of her sinking.

The Navy ship suffered no appreciable damage from the collision and stood by to offer aid. Called out from Portland, the Coast Guard tug *Yankton* appeared and towed the lightship to the Maine State Pier. An emergency replacement buoy was rushed to the lightship's normal position, where it served until a relief lightship, No. 89, showed up from Boston on the 15th.

A short time later, the Coast Guard announced that the useful days for No. 90 were nearly finished. Already more than forty years old, the second *Portland* had already outlived her predicted length of service by some fifteen years. Late in August 1952, she left her post a final time and sailed to Boston to be decommissioned.

On the date of No. 90's departure, her successor had yet to be named, so a relief

Portland Evening Express

WLV-536 served as *Portland* from 1969 to 1971. Here she is shown alongside the Coast Guard wharf at South Portland in September 1970 during her first visit to a Maine port.

ship, WAL-536 (or No. 114, as she originally had been called) stood on her station. On September 30, 1952, Coast Guard District Headquarters confirmed that Lightship WAL-533 (No. 111), built in Bath, Maine in 1926, had been assigned as the next Portland lightship. A product of the Bath Iron Works, the newest *Portland* was being transferred to Maine from New York, where she had just served a twenty-year span as the Ambrose lightship, at the entrance to New York Harbor. Previous to that, she had worked six years as *Northeast*, standing just off the northeast end of Five Fathom Bank, New Jersey.

Although the Bath Iron Works has enjoyed a long, successful history building ships for the U. S. government, the yard only once was involved in the construction of lightships. During the early 1920's it received a contract to provide six such vessels — numbers 106 through 111 — which it launched between 1923 and 1926.

At first glance, WAL-533 looked very much the same as her precursor, measuring 132 feet long, with a thirty-foot beam and a fourteen-foot draft. But unlike No. 90, the third *Portland* was a diesel-powered craft, rating a 450-horsepower engine. She displaced 780 tons and was capable of making eight knots. WAL-533 arrived in Portland during mid-October 1952, carrying most of the same crew that had served aboard No. 90. Boatswain Timothy P. Callaghan, skipper of the older vessel, commanded the newer boat as well.

After less than two years of duty, WAL-533 was taken to the Coast Guard base in South Portland, action prompted by repeated complaints from both mariners and harbor pilots who stated they couldn't hear her fog horn until they were "right on top of the vessel," preventing them from taking a safe berth while passing her. After conducting numerous tests, the Coast Guard installed larger air pipes and relocated No. 533's horn, enabling its throaty blare to be audible as much as three miles, even during the heaviest weather.

U.S. Coast Guard

WLV-612 was the fifth and last vessel to become the Portland lightship, a post she held from 1971 until 1975. Active since 1951, she spent her first twenty years on west coast stations, initially as *San Francisco*.

The decade of the 1960's witnessed the beginning of wholesale Coast Guard-efforts to retire the twenty-plus lightships remaining in active service by replacing them with automated navigational aids. Beginning in 1961, it tried the "Texas Tower," a giant platform-style structure standing on three or four steel-pile legs. By 1967, it was experimenting almost exclusively with what it called large navigational buoys, or LNB's for short. These were huge, cylindrical floating decks, bristling with electronic gear and surmounted by brilliant, winking lights.

These impersonal, though highly-efficient devices had won high praise from most quarters because they were able to carry out all the duties of lightships, including the transmission of weather and ocean data, without human assistance, therefore at far less expense. And since their operating costs were only a small fraction of those of manned lightships, these electronic robots were destined to become more and more prominent as offshore aids. The die had at last been cast, and now it was only a matter of time before the lightship would become a relic of the past.

Opposite: During the summer of 1971, WLV-612 was transferred to Portland. En route, she bent her propellor shaft off the west coast of Mexico and had to be towed to Colon, Panama, where she was hauled into dry dock for inspection and repairs.

Collection: Peter Dow Bachelder

During the summer of 1960, the government announced that the Portland lightship would be replaced by a Texas Tower. The change, it was said, would occur as soon as a suitable spot could be found to place it. Subsequent exploration of the ocean floor off Cape Elizabeth revealed a predominantly sand, mud, or clay bottom and the lack of extensive ledge formations. The latter was necessary to suitably anchor the tower's lanky legs. With these unfavorable findings, the government quietly shelved the idea of a tower.

In January 1964, the concept of a replacement tower surfaced again, although this time its design more closely resembled the still-experimental platform buoy. Once again, nothing positive resulted. Lack of money was claimed to be the determining factor, as was the uncertainty of how firmly such a structure could be planted.

Throughout her tour of duty off Cape Elizabeth, No. 533's annual maintenance checks were carried out in Boston, while a relief vessel from that port stood replacement duty. In October 1968, however, the forty-two year old lightvessel spent her "vacation" at the Coast Guard wharf in South Portland. While ashore, news broke that this would be the lightship's final inspection check — the *Portland* would be retired the following summer. Her replacement would not be a buoy or a Texas Tower, as most had surmised, but the Pollock Rip lightship. On the other hand, the Pollock Rip station would receive a buoy, further reducing the lightship flotilla.

Pollock Rip was in many ways similar to *Portland*. Built in 1930 at Portland, Oregon, she was of the same basic design as No. 533. Originally called No. 114, subsequently WLV-536, she had come to the east coast at the outset of her career, to be stationed off Fire Island, New York. During World War II, she was moved south to Diamond Shoal, North Carolina, often termed the most dangerous location on the Atlantic coast. Later she served for a time as a relief vessel, out of Boston, before ending up at Pollock Rip, southeast of Cape Cod.

As scheduled, the transfer of vessels occurred in July 1969. No. 536 moved into position off the harbor as No. 533 slipped into retirement. Instead of being decommissioned, the departing lightship gained a new lease on life when she was sold to the Uruguayan government for duty as the Banco Ingles lightship in that South American country.

By 1970, the process of lightship replacement with large navigational buoys was in high gear. As additional buoys were completed, they were assigned duty stations. In a number of instances, the displaced lightship, instead of being retired, would in turn replace an older, sister ship. No. 536 fell victim to these circumstances after barely more than two years off Cape Elizabeth. During the spring of 1971, it was announced that *Portland* would soon be relieved by another ship, one from the west coast.

This latest *Portland* was of a still more modern genre. She was WLV-612, one built at the U. S. Coast Guard yard, Curtis Bay, Maryland in 1950. Assigned to the Pacific coast, she arrived there in 1951 and served initially as the San Fran-

Guy Gannett Publishing Co.

The new red-and-white large navigational buoy (LNB), built to replace the Portland light-ship, arrives at the U.S. Coast Guard base in South Portland prior to being towed to its station off Cape Elizabeth.

cisco lightship, on a station eleven miles west of the Golden Gate Bridge. In 1969, she was redesignated Blunts Reef lightship and took up service four miles off Cape Mendocino, California. On June 9, 1971, she was succeeded by an LNB, whereupon she was assigned to Portland.

WLV-612 was 128 feet long, with a thirty-foot beam and an eleven-foot draft. Diesel-powered, she displaced 600 tons and possessed a cruising range of 22,000 miles, with a top speed of 11.5 knots.

The transfer of the Blunts Reef lightship from California to Maine left only two Pacific coast lightship stations — one at Umatilla Reef, off the Oregon coast; the other at the mouth of the Columbia River, between Washington and Oregon. The New Orleans lightship, in the Gulf of Mexico, and the Five Fathom Bank, Boston, Nantucket, and Portland lightships, along the eastern seaboard, were the only others in operation. In the three years since 1968, active U. S. lightships had dwindled from eighteen to seven.

WLV-612 left California on June 26, 1971 for what was expected to be a routine trip. A few days later, off Mexico's west coast she suffered a broken propeller shaft. Towed inshore to Salina Cruz by a Mexican Navy minesweeper, she was later taken in tow by the U.S.S. *Molala* for a 1,080-mile pull to Rodman, in the Panama Canal Zone. Following repairs and further inspections at Colon, Panama, she cleared the Panama Canal and turned north toward New England, arriving in Boston Harbor August 23, barely ahead of tropical storm Doria.

Meanwhile, off Portland, the threat of high winds and rough seas from Doria had prompted the removal of No. 536 from her station. Because No. 612 had been expected shortly, No. 536 headed to Boston for decommissioning after the storm passed. Unexpectedly, refitting chores aboard No. 612 consumed more time in Boston than anticipated, and Portland's harbor approaches went without any lightship for a month. On September 23, No. 612 arrived to take up her station, the fifth vessel to become the Portland lightship.

As modern and efficient as she was, WLV-612's days as *Portland* were numbered from the very beginning. With Coast Guard replacement of lightships with LNB's continuing throughout the service, it was only a question of time until the Portland station came up for changeover. In fact, that eventuality occurred little more than three years later. In January 1975, the Coast Guard released word that within the next few months, both the Portland and Boston lightships would be replaced by buoys. The move would reduce to two the remaining active duty lightships — the Nantucket and the Columbia River vessels.

Reaction to the announcement regarding *Portland's* retirement was somewhat

Portland leaves her station February 28, 1975 after having been replaced by a large navigational buoy. The buoy was constructed at the Bath Iron Works in Bath, Maine and weighed nearly 10.5 tons. Forty feet in diameter and 7.5 feet deep, it supported a 41-foot tower that showed a 75,000 candlepower light, a fog signal and a radiobeacon antenna.

U.S. Coast Guard

mixed. Generally speaking, most waterfront observers accepted it as just another step along the road of progress. Even among those not wanting to see the familiar ship go, the feeling was essentially tied to the kinds of sentiments felt at the parting of old friends.

Arnold Chandler, who had served more than two years aboard the *Portland*, commented: "Today, everything is automated. Why does everything have to be automated? You can have feeling for a ship. She was a good ship." Captain Charles C. "Sandy" Dunbar, president of the Portland Pilots Association, added: "We're going to miss the lightship and her crew, the personal contacts with the ship, the fine rapport we have enjoyed. We pilots have a tremendous affection for her." When asked for his feelings about the LNB, Dunbar remarked, "If the masters of incoming ships find it satisfactory, that's what counts."

From the Coast Guard's perspective, the LNB represented a new generation of markers for marine traffic, a breakthrough that revolutionized the type of offshore navigational aid that had stood the tests of time for more than 150 years. Economically speaking, the LNB was a godsend. In the first place, it greatly reduced personnel costs. Lightships required crews of fifteen to nineteen men, as well as support personnel ashore. LNB's were unmanned — their systems controlled and monitored from shore via UHF radio. Secondarily, LNB's were less expensive to build. The earliest light-vessels had cost less than $20,000 each, but by the 1970's, Coast Guard engineers estimated the cost of a modern lightship at approximately three million dollars. An LNB could be built for roughly one-sixth of that.

An early contract for LNB construction had been awarded to the Convair Division of General Dynamics, Inc., which in turn subcontracted work to the Bath Iron Works. Thus it came as a pleasant surprise to many local residents when they learned that Portland's LNB was "Maine-made" — a reassuring fact, since Maine people have long held a rightful sense of pride for the quality of work turned out by the renowned Bath firm. BIW had constructed seven working LNB's during 1970 and 1971. Under the contract that produced the Portland buoy, Bath was also building another to replace the Boston lightship, as well as a third for use as back up for the former pair.

February 26, 1975 had been targeted as Portland Harbor's changeover date from lightship to LNB, but when that day arrived, accompanied by strong, gusty winds and rough seas, it was deemed too risky to undertake the meticulous task of placing the big buoy on her prescribed station. The LNB would be held in place by a ten-ton sinker and attached anchor cable. On-site seas would have to be relatively calm to allow a buoy tender to hold its position during the delicate setting procedure.

Marginal conditions continued for another day, further delaying the operation. But February 28 dawned sparkling clear and calm, presenting almost perfect conditions for the historic occasion. The Coast Guard buoy tender *Spar* churned seaward from Portland's inner harbor, reaching a spot near the red-hulled lightship shortly before noontime. The *Spar's* crew soon had the LNB's gigantic anchor in the water, then began the slow-motion task of paying out the links of chain. Because of the anchor's tremendous weight, the chain was let out one link at a time, resulting in an almost three-hour period before the great weight was resting firmly on the ocean floor, nearly 160 feet below the surface.

About forty-five minutes before the *Spar* completed the anchor-lowering procedure, the tug *Yankton* arrived, towing the curious-looking LNB well behind, the latter looking very much like a giant candle stuck in a dish. By two-thirty in the afternoon, the hookup of buoy and chain had been accomplished. With that, the lightship hauled her own big mushroom and turned her bow toward Portland Harbor. It was all over. Lacking exactly one week of completing its seventy-second year, the era of the Portland lightship had ended forever.

BIBLIOGRAPHY

PRIMARY MATERIAL

Records

Two basic collections of government documents provide the best primary information on American lighthouses and lightships — in fact, on the establishment and development of the country's entire system of navigational aids. They are the *Congressional Serial Set*, which can be found in many major libraries. and *Record Group 26*, housed in the National Archives, Washington, D.C.

The Serial Set comprises the ongoing, printed business record of the nation's two federal legislative bodies, the U.S. Senate and the House of Representatives. Liberally sprinkled throughout this voluminous holding, dating from 1789, are countless diverse but extremely illuminating documents of prime interest and utility to those researching lighthouse history — locally initiated letters, petitions, and reports sent to Washington from civic-minded citizens, groups, and businesses trying to prompt additional or improved navigational aids; annual reports from various boards, departments, and agencies, such as the Department of War, the Secretary of the Treasury, the U.S. Coast Survey, et al., which sometimes include circulars, directives, and other correspondence to field representatives requesting navigation-related studies or similar initiatives. The often-detailed responses to these called-for activities frequently combine insightful information complemented by skillfully prepared maps, plates, charts, and other supporting data.

Also found in the set are in-depth reports made in response to congressionally-ordered inspections and probes. These include the ones authorized in 1838, and again in 1851, which thoroughly delved into the workings of the entire lighthouse establishment, its personnel and equipment, as well as its management operations and strategies. Here, too, are occasional annual reports of the U.S. Light-House Board, organized in 1852; reviews, accounts, and recommendations concerning technological advances and improvements in navigational aids, and proposed changes to the system's administrative hierarchy and governing practices.

Record Group 26, Records of the U.S.Coast Guard (and its predecessor agencies), contains the surviving correspondence, journals, contract abstracts, personnel ledgers, site files, and more, for each individual light station and lightship.

SECONDARY MATERIAL

Books

Annual Reports of the Light House Board to the Secretary of the Treasury, 1852–1910. Washington, D.C.: U.S. Government Printing Office.

Attwood, Stanley B., *The Length and Breadth of Maine*, Augusta: Kennebec Journal Print Shop, 1946.

Drake, Samuel Adams, *Nooks and Corners of the New England Coast*, New York: Harper and Bros., 1875.

—, *The Pine Tree Coast*, Boston: Estes & Lauriat, 1890.

Goold, William, *Portland in the Past*, Portland: B. Thurston & Co., 1886.

Heap, David Porter, *Ancient and Modern Lighthouses*, Boston: Ticknor & Co., 1889.

Jordan, William B., *A History of Cape Elizabeth*, Maine, Portland: House of Falmouth, 1965.

Journals of the Rev. Thomas Smith and the Rev. Samuel Deane, Pastors of the First Church in Portland, with Notes and a Summary History of Portland, Portland: Joseph S. Bailey, 1849.

Perley, Sidney, *Historic Storms of New England*, Salem, Mass., 1891.

Putnam, George R., *Lighthouses and Lightships of the United States*, Boston: Houghton Mifflin Co., 1917.

—, *Sentinels of the Coast; The Log of a Lighthouse Engineer*, New York: W. W. Norton & Co., 1937.

Rowe, William Hutchinson, *The Maritime History of Maine*, New York: W. W. Norton & Co., 1948.

—, *Shipbuilding Days in Casco Bay, being footnotes to the Maritime History of Maine*, Yarmouth, 1929.

Snow, Edward Rowe, *Famous New England Lighthouses*, Boston: Yankee Publishing Co., 1945.

—, *Storms and Shipwrecks of New England*, Boston: Yankee Publishing Co., 1943.

Sterling, Robert Thayer, *Lighthouses of the Maine Coast and the Men Who Keep Them*, Brattleboro, Vt.: Stephen Daye Press, 1935.

Talbot, Frederick A., *Lightships and Lighthouses*, Philadelphia: J. B. Lippincott Co., 1913.

U. S. Light-House Board, *List of Lights and Fog Signals of the Atlantic and Gulf Coasts of the United States*, Washington: U. S. Government Printing Office, 1852, 1893, 1925, 1970, 1993.

Willard, Captain Benjamin J., *Captain Ben's Book*, Portland: Lakeside Press, 1895.

Williamson, Joseph, *A Bibliography of the State of Maine from the Earliest Period to 1891*, Portland: Thurston Printing, 1896.

Willis, William, *The History of Portland; a facsimile of the 1865 edition with a new forward by Gerald Morris*, Somersworth, N. H.: New Hampshire Publishing, 1972.

Willoughby, Malcolm F., *Lighthouses of New England*, Boston T. O. Metcalf Co., 1929.

Maine Newspapers

Portland (Maine) *Cumberland Gazette*
— *Eastern Argus*
— *Eastern Herald and Gazette of Maine*
— *Eastern Herald and Maine Gazette*
— *Falmouth Gazette Weekly Advertiser*
— *Portland Advertiser*
— *Portland Daily Press*
— *Portland Evening Express*
— *Portland Press Herald*
— *Portland Sunday Telegram*
— *Portland Times*
— *Portland Transcript*

INDEX

THE LIGHTHOUSES & LIGHTSHIPS OF CASCO BAY was set in 11 point Bell Monotype, which is based on the original types designed by John Bell in 1788. It is printed on 60 lb. Lakewood Offset, acid-free paper by Bookcrafters of Chelsea, Michigan. The book was designed and published by The Provincial Press, Portland, Maine.

OTHER PROVINCIAL PRESS BOOKS

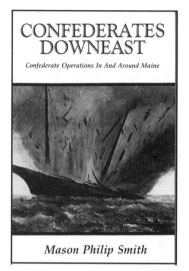